SAY IT IN NORWEGIAN

BY

SAMUEL ABRAHAMSEN, Ph.D.

D0828094

Dover Publications, Inc.

New York

Published in Canada by General Publishing Company, Ltd., 30 Lesmill Road, Don Mills, Toronto, Ontario.

Published in the United Kingdom by Constable and Company, Ltd., 10 Orange Street, London WC 2.

Standard Book Number: 486-20814-1
Library of Congress Catalog Card Number: 57-36629

Manufactured in the United States of America
Dover Publications, Inc.
180 Varick Street
New York, N.Y. 10014

CONTENTS

CONTENTS

INTRODUCTION

SAY IT IN NORWEGIAN makes available to you, in simple usable form, all the words and sentences you need for travel and everyday living in Norway. The given English phrases are those shown by experience to be the most needed. The translations are idiomatic rather than literal, for your primary goal is to make yourself understood. The Norwegian words are pronounced for you in a simple phonetic system explained below.

Since 1896 Norway has had three spelling reforms. SAY IT IN NORWEGIAN follows that of 1938 along lines drawn up by Sverdrup and Sandvei in *Norsk Rettskrivningsordbok* (Oslo, 1953).

Sentence Structure

No attempt is made to teach the grammatical structure of Norwegian, but almost every phrase and sentence is complete in itself and can be used without knowledge of grammar. However, you will discover that Norwegian sentences are constructed in much the same way as English; the two languages are in fact closely related. As your vocabulary increases, you will find that you can construct many additional sentences of your own. To avoid grammatical error in this process, take note of the genders of nouns. The two principal genders are common (*c.*) and neuter (*n.*). Common nouns take the article *en*; neuter nouns take the article *et*. Certain nouns are denoted as masculine (*m.*) as *en mann* or feminine (*f.*) as *ei kone*; in modern Norwegian almost all such nouns are treated grammatically as of common gender.

The Index

You will find the extensive index in the back of this book especially helpful. Note that most of the references are to *entry numbers*, not to pages. The only exceptions are the capitalized items, which are section headings; the first reference after each such item, labeled "p. oo" is to the page number.

The primary purpose of the index is of course to enable you to locate quickly the specific word or phrase you need at the moment. But it can do more for you. If you will compare the various passages in which the same root-word occurs, you will discover a great deal about its inflexional forms. You will also discover synonyms and otherwise related words.

Pronunciation

The phonetic transcription is based on the spoken language in South-eastern Norway (Oslo), which is the dialect used most frequently by the newspapers, heard most often on the radio, in Parliament, and in the classroom. The language in SAY IT IN NORWEGIAN is known variously as "Riksmål" or "Bokmål" (State or Book Language) which is spoken by most people in Norway.

Pronounce the phonetic transcriptions as though they were English text, with due regard for those few Norwegian sounds which do not exist in English. Do not memorize the table below—though you will do well to read through it once. Try pronouncing half a dozen of the phrases, then check yourself by the table. You will quickly find that you have learned the scheme and need refer again to the table only rarely.

SAMUEL ABRAHAMSEN, PH.D.

Transcription	*Pronunciation*

Vowels

ă	as *a* in *cat*.
ah	as *a* in *father*.
aw	as *aw* in *awful*.
ay	as *ay* in *day*.
e	as *e* in *let*.
ee	as *ee* in *feed*.
eh	as *e* in *the* (this is the "mute e" of French, German and other languages).
e̲w̲	as *ew* in *new*.
e̅w̅	as *u* in French *rue*. (This sound does not exist in English. Purse the lips as though to pronounce *oo* but say *ee*.)
e̅r̅	as *e* in *her* BUT DO NOT PRONOUNCE THE *r* unless a second *r* follows (this is the same as *eu* in French *peu*).
i	as *i* in *sit*.
oh	as *o* in *note*.
oo	as *oo* in *tool*.
oy	as *oy* in *boy*.
u	as *u* in *cut*.

Consonants

ch	as *ch* in German *ich*. (This sound does not exist in English. It is intermediate between *ik* and *ish*.)
g	as *g* in *go*.
ng	as *ng* in *sing*
r	trill with the tip of the tongue.
s, ss	as *s* in *set*.
sh	as *sh* in *show*.

All other consonants are pronounced (in whatever combinations they occur) as in English.
The other consonants used in the phonetic transcription are:

b, d, f, h, k, l, m, n, p, t, v.

USEFUL EXPRESSIONS

NYTTIGE UTTRYKK

1. Yes. No. Perhaps.
Ja. Nei. Kanskje.
yah. nay. KAHN-sheh.

2. Please.
Vær så snill.
VÄR saw snil.

3. Excuse me.
Unnskyld.
EWN-shewl.

4. Help me.
Hjelp meg.
yelp may.

5. Thanks (very much).
Takk (tusen takk).
TAHK (TEW-sen TAHK).

6. You are welcome.
Ingen årsak OR: Vær så god.
ING-en AW-shahk OR: VÄR saw GOO.

7. Does anyone here speak English?
Snakker man engelsk her?
SNUK-keh mahn ENG-elsk HÄR?

8. I speak only English (French).
Jeg snakker bare engelsk (fransk).
yay SNUK-keh BAH-reh ENG-elsk (FRAHNSK).

9. I know a little German (Italian, Spanish).
Jeg kan litt tysk (italiensk, spansk).
yay KAHN lit TEWSK (ee-TAH-lee-ensk, SPAHNSK).

9

10. I am an American citizen.
Jeg er amerikansk borger.
yay är ah-meh-ree-KAHNSK BAWR-gehr.

11. I do not understand.
Jeg forstår ikke.
yay fawr-STAWR IK-eh.

12. Repeat it, please.
Vær så snill å gjenta.
VÄR saw snil aw YEN-tah.

13. Write it down, please.
Vær så snill og skriv det ned.
VÄR saw snil aw SKREEV deh neh.

14. Once more. The address.
En gang til. Adressen.
EN-GAHNG til. ah-DRESS-en.

15. The Date. The Number.
Datoen. Nummeret.
DAH-too-en. NOOM-eh-reh.

16. The time.
Klokka OR: Tiden.
KLUK-ah OR: TEE-din.

17. What time is it?
Hva er klokka?
vah är KLUK-ah?

18. I have plenty of time.
Jeg har god tid.
yay HAHR goo tee.

19. I am having a good time.
Jeg har det moro.
yay hahr deh MOO-roh.

20. How do you say ——?
Hvordan sier De ——?
VOOR-dahn SEE-ehr dee ——?

21. What is this called in ——?
Hva heter dette på ——?
vah HAY-tehr DET-eh paw ——?

22. My name is ——.
Jeg heter —— OR: mitt navn er ——.
yay HAY-tehr —— OR: mit NAH-ven är ——.

23. I spell my name thus: ——.
Jeg staver mitt navn slik: ——.
yay STAH-vehr mit NAH-ven shleek: ——.

24. My (mailing) address is ——.
Min (post) adresse er ——.
meen (POHST) ah-DRESS-eh är ——.

25. Please speak more slowly.
Vær så snill og snakk langsommere.
VÄR saw snil aw SNUK LAHNG-sawm-eh-reh.

26. What do you wish?
Hva ønsker De?
vah ERN-skehr DEE?

27. Where is (are)?
Hvor er?
voor ÄR?

28. Wait a moment.
Vent et øyeblikk.
VENT et OY-eh-BLIK.

29. How much is it?
Hvor mye koster det?
voor MEW-eh KAWST-eh deh?

30. It is old (new).
Den er gammel (ny).
den är GAHM-el (NEW).

31. It is (it is not) all right.
Det er (det er ikke) bra.
deh är (deh är IK-eh) BRAH.

32. That is (that is not) all.
Det er (det er ikke) alt.
deh är (deh är IK-eh) AHLT.

33. Why? Hvorfor? *VOOR-fawr?*

34. When? Når? *nawr?*

35. How? Hvordan? *VOOR-dahn?*

36. How far? Hvor langt? *voor LAHNGT?*

37. How long? Hvor lenge? *voor LENG-eh?*

38. Who? Hvem? *vem?*

39. What? Hva? *vah?*

40. Here. Her. *hăr.*

41. There. Der. *dăr.*

42. To. Til. *til.*

43. From. Fra. *frah.*

44. With. Med. *meh.*

45. Without. Foruten. *fawr-EW-ten.*

46. In. I. *ee.*

47. On. På. *paw.*

48. Near. Nær. *nǎr.*

49. Far. Langt. *lahngt.*

50. In front of. Foran. *FAWR-ahn.*

51. Behind. Bak. *bahk.*

52. Beside. Ved siden av. *veh SEE-dehn ahv.*

53. Inside. Innafor. *EEN-ah-FAWR.*

54. Outside. Utafor. *EW-tah-FAWR.*

55. Something. Noenting. *NOON-ting.*

56. Nothing. Ingenting. *EENG-en-ting.*

57. Several. Flere. *FLAY-reh.*

58. Few. Få. *faw.*

59. Enough. Nok. *nawk.*

60. Too much. (Alt) for mye.
(*AHLT-*) *fawr MEW-eh.*

61. (Much) more (quantity). **Most.**
(Mye) mere. Mest.
(*MEW-eh*) *MEH-reh.   mest.*

62. Many. Mange. *MAHN-geh.*

63. More (number). Flere. *FLAY-reh.*

64. Most (number). Flest. *flest.*

65. A little. Litt. *lit.*

66. Less. Mindre. *MIN-dreh.*

67. Least. Minst. *minst.*

68. Empty. Tom. *toom.*

69. Full. Full. *fewl.*

70. Good. God. *goo.*

71. Better (than). Bedre (enn).
 BEH-dreh (en).

72. Best. Best. *best.*

73. Bad. Dårlig. *DAW-lee.*

74. Worse (than). Verre (enn). *VÅR-reh (en).*

75. Again. Igjen. *ee-YEN.*

76. Also. Også. *AW-saw.*

77. Now. Nå. *naw.*

78. Immediately. Straks. *strahks.*

79. Soon. Snart. *snahrt.*

80. As soon as possible. Så snart som mulig.
 saw snahrt sawm MEW-lee.

81. Later. Senere. *SAY-neh-reh.*

82. Slowly. Langsom. *LAHNG-sawm.*

83. Slower. Langsommere. *LAHNG-sawm-eh-reh.*

84. Quickly. Fort. *foort.*

85. Faster. Fortere. *FOORT-eh-reh.*

86. Come here. Kom hit. *kawm heet.*

87. Come in. Kom inn. *kawm in.*

88. It is early.
Det er tidlig.
deh är TEE-lee.

89. It is (too) late.
Det er (for) sent.
deh är (fawr) saynt.

90. Men's room. Ladies' room.
Menn OR: Herrer. Kvinner OR: Damer.
men OR: HÄR-ehr. KVEEN-ehr OR: DAHM-ehr.

91. I am warm. I am cold.
Jeg er varm. Jeg fryser.
yay är VAHRM. yay FREW-sehr.

92. I am hungry (thirsty, sleepy).
Jeg er sulten (tørst, søvnig).
yay är SEWL-ten (TERSHT, SERV-nee).

93. I am (not) in a hurry.
Jeg har det (ikke) travelt.
yay hahr deh (IK-eh) TRAH-velt.

94. I am busy (tired, ill).
Jeg er opptatt (trett, sjuk).
yay är AWP-taht (tret, shewk).

95. I am lost.
Jeg har gått meg bort.
yay hahr gawt may boort.

96. I am looking for ——.
Jeg søker ——.
yay SERK-ehr ——.

97. I am glad (sorry).
Jeg er glad (bedrøvet).
yay är glah (beh-DRĒRV-et).

98. I am ready.
Jeg er ferdig.
yay är FÄR-ee.

99. Can you tell me ——?
Kan De si meg ——?
kahn dee see MAY ——?

100. What is that?
Hva er det?
vah är deh?

101. I should like ——.
Jeg vil gjerne ha ——.
yay vil YÄR-neh hah ——.

102. Can you recommend ——?
Kan De anbefale ——?
kahn dee AHN-beh-FAH-leh ——?

103. Do you want ——?
Ønsker De ——?
ĒRN-skehr dee ——?

104. I (do not) know.
Jeg vet (ikke).
yay vet (IK-eh).

105. I (do not) think so.
Jeg tror (ikke) det.
yay troor (IK-eh) deh.

106. I beg your pardon.
Om forlatelse.
awm fawr-LAHT-el-seh.

107. I cannot find my hotel address.

Jeg kan ikke finne min hoteladresse.

yay kahn IK-eh FIN-eh meen hoo-TEL-ah-DRESS-eh.

108. I do not remember the street.

Jeg husker ikke gata.

yay HEW-skeh IK-eh GAHT-ah.

109. I have lost my friends.

Jeg har mistet mine venner.

yay hahr MIST-et MEEN-eh VEN-eh.

110. I left my purse (wallet) in the ——.

Jeg glemte igjen min pung (lommebok) i ——.

yay GLEM-teh ee-YEN meen poong (LOOM-eh-bohk) ee ——.

111. I forgot my money (keys).

Jeg glemte igjen pengene mine (nøklene mine).

yay GLEM-teh ee-YEN PENG-eh-neh MEEN-eh (NERK-leh-neh MEEN-eh).

112. I have missed my train (plane, bus).

Jeg kom for sent til toget (flyet, bussen).

yay kawm fawr saynt til TAW-geh (FLEW-eh, BEWSS-en).

113. What is the matter here?

Hva er på ferde?

vah är paw FÄR-eh?

114. What shall I do?

Hva skal jeg gjøre?

vah skah yay YER-reh?

115. It is (not) my fault.

Det er (ikke) min skyld.

deh är (IK-eh) meen SHEWL.

116. They are bothering me.
De plager meg.
dee PLAH-geh may.

117. Go away!
Gå bort!
gaw boort!

118. Where is the American consul?
Hvor er den amerikanske konsul?
voor är den AH-meh-ree-KAHNSK-eh KAWN-sewl?

119. I will call a policeman.
Jeg skal tilkalle en politikonstabel.
yay skahl TIL-kahl-eh en poo-lee-TEE-koon-STAH-bel.

120. Where is the police station?
Hvor er politistasjonen?
voor är poo-lee-TEE-stah-SHOON-en?

121. I have been robbed of ——.
Jeg er frastjålet ——.
yay är FRAH-styaw-let ——.

122. The lost and found office.
Hittegodskontoret.
HIT-eh-goos-koon-TOOR-eh.

123. Help! Fire! Thief!
Hjelp! Brann! Tyv!
yelp! brahn! tewv!

124. Look (out)! Stop! Listen!
Se (opp)! Stopp! Hør!
seh (awp)! stawp! herr!

GREETINGS AND INTRODUCTIONS

HILSNING OG PRESENTASJON

125. Good morning.   Good evening.
God morgen.   God kveld (OR: aften).
goo MAWRN.   goo KVEL (OR: AHF-ten).

126. Hello.   Goodbye.
God dag.   Adjø.
goo-DAH.   ah-DYER.

127. I'll be seeing you.
På gjensyn.
paw YEN-sewn.

128. What is your name?
Hva heter De? OR: Hva er Deres navn?
vah HAY-teh dee? OR: vah är DAY-ress NAH-ven?

129. May I introduce Mr. (Mrs., Miss) ——?
Må jeg få presentere herr (fru, frøken) ——?
maw yay faw PREH-sen-TEH-reh här (frew, FRER-ken) ——?

130. My wife.   Min kone (OR: frue).
meen KOON-eh (OR: FREW-eh).

131. My husband.   Min mann.   *meen mahn.*

132. My daughter.   Min datter.
meen DAHT-ter.

133. My son.   Min sønn.   *meen sern.*

134. My friend.   Min venn.   *meen ven.*

135. My relative.   Min slektning.
meen SHLEKT-neeng.

136. My sister.   Min søster.   *meen SERS-tehr.*

137. My brother. Min bror. *meen BROOR.*

138. I am a friend of Mr. ——.
Jeg er venn av herr ——.
yay ăr ven ahv hăr ——.

139. I am happy to make your acquaintance.
Det gleder meg å treffe Dem.
deh GLAY-deh may aw TREF-eh dem.

140. Pleased to meet you.
Det var hyggelig å møte Dem.
deh vahr HEWG-eh-lee aw MER-teh dem.

141. How are you?
Hvordan står det til?
VOOR-dahn STAWR deh TIL?

142. Fine, thanks; and you?
Bare bra, takk; og med Dem?
BAH-reh BRAH, tahk ; aw meh dem?

143. How is your family?
Hvordan står det til med Deres familie?
VOOR-dahn STAWR deh til meh DAY-ress fah-MEEL-yeh?

144. (Not very) well.
(Ikke så) bra.
(IK-keh saw) brah.

145. Please sit down.
Vær så god og sitt ned.
văr saw goo aw sit neh.

146. I have enjoyed myself very much.
Jeg har hatt det veldig hyggelig.
yay hahr hut deh VEL-dee HEWG-eh-lee.

147. I hope to see you again soon.

Jeg håper vi treffes snart igjen.

yay HAWP-eh vee TREF-ess snahrt ee-YEN.

148. Come to see me (us).

Kom og besøk meg (oss).

KAWM aw beh-SERK may (awss).

149. Give me your address (and telephone number).

La meg få Deres adresse (og telefon-nummer).

lah may faw DAY-ress ah-DRESS-eh (aw teh-leh-FOON-noom-eh).

150. Give my regards to ——.

Gi mine hilsener til —— OR: Hils til ——.

YEE meen-eh HEELSS-eh-neh til —— OR: HEELSS til ——.

151. We are travelling to ——.

Vi skal reise til ——.

vee skah RAY-seh til ——.

152. (Heartiest) congratulations.

Gratulerer (hjerteligst).

grah-tew-LEHR-er (YÅR-teh-ligst).

153. Happy Birthday!

Gratulerer med fødselsdagen!

grah-tew-LEHR-er meh FERDS-els-dah-en!

154. Merry Christmas!

Gledelig jul!

GLAY-deh-lee YEWL.

155. Happy New Year!

Godt nytt år!

GAWT NEWT awr!

156. Bon Voyage!
God tur!
Goo TEWR!

157. May I have a date with you for tomorrow evening?
Kan jeg møte Dem i morgen kveld?
kahn yay MER-teh dem ee-MAWRN kvel?

TRAVEL: GENERAL EXPRESSIONS

REISE: ALMINNELIGE UTTRYKK

158. Can you direct me to a travel agency (an airline office)?
Kan De si meg veien til et reisekontor (flyselskapets kontor)?
kahn dee see may VAY-en til et RAY-seh-koon-TOOR (FLEW-sel-SKAHP-ets koon-TOOR)?

159. I want to go to the airport (bus station).
Jeg skal til flyplassen (busstasjonen).
yay skah til FLEW-plahss-en (BEWSS-stah-shoon-en).

160. Is the railroad station near here?
Er jernbanestasjonen i nærheten?
är YÄRN-bahn-en-stah-SHOON-en ee NÄR-het-en?

161. What is the best way of traveling?
Hva er den beste måten å reise på?
vah är den BEST-eh MAWT-en aw RAY-seh paw?

162. How long will it take to go to ——?
Hvor lenge vil det ta å reise til ——?
voor LENG-eh vil deh tah aw RAY-seh til ——?

163. When will we arrive at ——?
Når vil vi komme til ——?
nawr vil vee KAWM-eh til ——?

164. Please get me a taxi.
Vær så snill å få tak i en drosje.
văr saw snil aw faw tahk ee en DRAW-sheh.

165. Where is the baggage room?
Hvor er ekspedisjonen?
voor är EKS-pay-dee-SHOON-en?

166. I need a porter.
Jeg trenger en bærer.
yay TRENG-ehr en BÄR-ehr.

167. Follow me, please.
Vær så snill og følg etter meg.
văr saw snil aw ferl ET-ter may.

168. Can I reserve a seat?
Kan jeg bestille plass?
kahn yay beh-STEEL-eh plahss?

169. I want a seat near the window.
Jeg vil ha en plass nær vinduet.
yay vil hah en plahss năr VEEN-dew-eh.

170. Is this seat taken?
Er denne plassen opptatt?
är DEN-eh PLAHSS-en AWP-taht?

171. Where is the nearest station?
Hvor er den nærmeste stasjonen?
voor är den năr-mest-eh stah-SHOON-en?

172. Is this the (direct) way to ——?
Er dette (direkte) veien til ——?
är DET-eh (dee-REK-teh) VAY-en til ——?

173. Which is the quickest?
Hvilken er fortest?
VEEL-ken är FOORT-est?

174. How does one go (there)?
Hvordan kommer man til (dit)?
VOOR-dahn KAWM-ehr mahn til (deet)?

175. Show me on the map.
Vis meg på kartet.
veess may paw KAHRT-eh.

176. Does it stop at ——?
Stopper det på ——?
STAWP-eh deh paw ——?

177. Is there a subway?
Er det en undergrunnsbane?
är deh en EWN-ner-grewnss-BAH-neh?

178. Where do I turn?
Hvor skal jeg ta av?
VOOR skah yay TAH ahv?

179. To the north. Til nord. *til noor.*

180. To the south. Til syd. *til sewd.*

181. To the east. Til øst. *til erst.*

182. To the west. Til vest. *til vest.*

183. To the right. Til høyre. *til HOY-reh.*

184. To the left. Til venstre. *til VENSS-treh.*

185. Straight ahead. Rett fram. *ret frahm.*

186. The corner. Hjørnet. *YER-neh.*

187. Forward. Framover. *FRAHM-aw-veh.*

188. Back. Tilbake. *til-BAH-keh.*

189. The Street. Gata. *GAH-tah.*

190. The Square. Torget. *TAWR-geh.*

191. The Place. Plassen. *PLAHSS-en.*

192. The Avenue. Avenyen. *ah-veh-NEW-en.*

193. The Road. Veien. *VAY-en.*

194. The Park. Parken. *PAHRK-en.*

195. Is this the right direction?
Er dette den riktige retningen?
är DET-eh den REEK-tee-eh RET-ning-en?

196. Please point!
Pek, er De snill!
PEK, är dee snil!

197. What street is this?
Hvilken gate er dette?
VEEL-ken GAH-teh är DET-eh?

198. Do I have to change (train, bus, plane)?
Må jeg bytte (tog, buss, fly)?
maw yay BEWT-eh (TAWG, BEWSS, FLEW)?

199. Please tell me where to get off.
Vær så snill å si meg hvor jeg skal gå av.
vär saw snil aw see may voor yay skahl gaw ahv.

AT THE CUSTOMS

PÅ TOLLBUA

200. Where is the customs?
Hvor er tollen?
voor år TAWL-en?

201. Here is my baggage, —— pieces.
Her er min bagasje, —— kolli.
hår år meen bah-GAH-sheh, —— KAWL-lee.

202. This package contains clothing (food, books).
Denne pakken inneholder klær (mat, bøker).
DEN-eh PAHK-en IN-neh-HAWL-ehr klår (MAHT, BĒRK-ehr).

203. Here is my passport (visa).
Her er mitt pass (visum).
hår år mit pahss (VEE-sewm).

204. I have my landing ticket.
Jeg har min landingsbillett.
yay hahr meen LAHN-ingss-bee-LET.

205. I am a tourist on vacation.
Jeg er turist på ferie.
yay år tew-REEST paw FEHR-yah.

206. This is a business visit.
Dette er et forretningsbesøk.
DET-eh år et fawr-RET-nings-beh-sērk.

207. I am in transit.
Jeg er på gjennomreise.
yay år paw YEN-oom-ray-seh.

208. Must I open everything?
Skal jeg åpne alt?
skahl yay AWP-neh ahlt?

209. I cannot open that.
Jeg kan ikke åpne den der.
yay kan IK-eh AWP-neh den dăr.

210. I have nothing to declare.
Jeg har ikke noe å fortolle.
yay hahr IK-eh NOO-eh aw fawr-TAWL-eh.

211. All this is for my personal use.
Alt dette er bare til personlig bruk.
ahlt DET-eh ăr BAH-reh til pehr-SOON-lee brewk.

212. There is nothing here but ——.
Det er ingenting her utenom ——.
deh ăr EENG-en-ting hăr EWT-en-oom ——.

213. These are gifts.
Dette er gaver.
DET-eh ăr GAHV-ehr.

214. Are these things dutiable?
Er det toll på disse tingene?
ăr deh TAWL paw DISS-eh TING-eh-neh?

215. How much must I pay?
Hvor mye må jeg betale?
voor MEW-eh maw yay beh-TAHL-eh?

216. This is all I have.
Det er alt jeg har.
deh ăr ahlt yay hahr.

217. Please be careful!
Vær forsiktig!
vär fawr-SHEEK-tee!

218. Have you finished?
Er De ferdig?
är dee FÄR-ee?

219. I cannot find my baggage.
Jeg kan ikke finne bagasjen min.
yay kahn IK-eh FIN-eh bah-GAH-shen meen.

220. My train leaves in —— minutes.
Toget mitt går om —— minutter.
TAW-geh mit gawr AWM —— mee-NEWT-er.

TICKETS

BILLETTER

221. Where is the ticket office?
Hvor er billettkontoret?
voor är bee-LET-koon-TOOR-eh?

222. I need a ticket (timetable) to ——.
Jeg skal ha billett (togtabell) til ——.
*yay skah hah bee-LET (TAWG-tah-BEL) til
——.*

223. How much is a one-way (round-trip) ticket to ——?
Hvor mye er enkelbillett (tur-retur) til ——?
voor MEW-eh är EN-kel-bee-LET (TEWR-ray-TEWR) til ——?

224. First (second) class.
Første (annen) klasse.
FERST-eh (AHN-en) KLAHSS-eh.

225. Is there an express (local) train to ——?
Er det et hurtigtog (lokaltog) til ——?
är deh et HEWR-tee-TAWG (loo-KAHL-TAWG) til ——?

226. A reserved seat, please.
En plassbillett, takk.
en PLAHSS-bee-let, TAHK.

227. Can I go by way of ——?
Kan jeg reise over ——?
kahn yay RAY-seh AWV-eh ——?

228. Is there a later (earlier) train?
Er det noe senere (tidligere) tog?
är deh NOO-eh SAY-neh-reh (TEE-lee-eh-reh) tawg?

229. From what station (platform) does the train leave?
Fra hvilken stasjon (perrong OR: spor) går toget?
frah VEEL-ken STAH-shoon (PAYR-awng OR: SPOOR) gawr TAWG-eh?

230. How long is this ticket good?
Hvor lenge gjelder billetten?
voor LENG-eh-YEL-eh bee-LET-en?

231. Can I get something to eat on the way?
Kan jeg få noe å spise på veien?
kahn yay faw NOO-eh aw SPEESS-eh paw VAY-en?

232. How much baggage may I take?
Hvor mye reisegods kan jeg ta med meg?
voor MEW-eh RAY-seh-goos kahn yay TAH meh may?

BAGGAGE

BAGASJE

233. Where can I check my baggage?
Hvor kan jeg ekspedere tøyet mitt?
voor kahn yay EKS-peh-deh-reh TOY-eh mit?

234. I want to leave these trunks for a while.
Jeg vil sette inn disse koffertene en stund.
yay vil SET-eh in DEESS-eh KOOF-ert-eh-neh en STEWN.

235. Do I pay now or later?
Skal jeg betale nå eller senere?
skah yay beh-TAHL-eh naw EL-eh SAY-neh-reh?

236. I want to take out my baggage.
Jeg vil hente tøyet mitt.
yay vil HAYN-teh TOY-eh mit.

237. Mine is over there.
Mitt er der borte.
mit är DÄR BOOR-teh.

238. Handle this very carefully.
Vær forsiktig med denne.
vär fawr-SEEK-tee meh DEN-eh.

239. Where can I find the stationmaster?
Hvor kan jeg finne stasjonsmesteren?
voor kan yay FIN-eh STAH-shoonss-MEST-eh-rɛn?

AIRPLANE

FLY

240. Is there bus service to the airport?
Går det buss til flyplassen?
gawr deh BEWSS til FLEW-plahss-en?

241. At what time will they come for me?
Når vil de hente meg?
nawr vil dee HENT-eh may?

242. When is there a plane to ——?
Når går et fly til ——?
nawr gawr et flew til ——?

243. What is the flight number?
Hvilket flynummer er det?
VEEL-ket FLEW-noom-er år deh?

244. Is food served on the plane?
Serveres det mat på flyet?
sär-VÄR-ess deh MAHT paw FLEW-eh?

245. How many kilos may I take?
Hvor mange kilo kan jeg ta med?
voor MAHNG-eh kyee-loh kahn yay tah meh?

246. How much per kilogram (pound) for excess?
Hvor mye per kilo (pund) i overvekt?
voor MEW-eh pår kyee-loh (pewn) ee AW-vehr-vekt?

247. Fasten your safety belts.
Ta på sikkerhetsbeltene.
tah paw SIK-ehr-hets-BELT-eh-neh.

BOAT

BÅT

248. Can I go by boat (ferry) to ——?
Kan jeg reise med båt (ferje) til ——?
kahn yay RAY-seh meh BAWT (FÄR-yeh) til——?

249. When does the next boat leave?
Når går neste båt?
nawr gawr NEST-eh BAWT?

250. When must I be on board?
Når må jeg gå om bord?
nawr maw yay gaw oom boor?

251. Can I land at ——?
Kan jeg gå i land i ——?
kahn yay gaw ee-LAHND ee ——?

252. The captain.   The officer.
Kapteinen.   Offiseren.
kahp-TAY-nen.   AW-fee-SAY-ren.

253. The deck.   Upper.   Lower.
Dekket.   Øvre.   Nedre.
DEK-eh. $\overline{ERV}$-reh.   NAY-dreh.

254. Where is the purser (steward)?
Hvor er intendenten (stuerten)?
voor är een-ten-DAHN-ten (STEW-ehrt-en)?

255. I want to rent a deck chair.
Jeg vil leie en dekkstol.
yay vil LAY-eh en DEK-stool.

256. I am seasick.
Jeg er sjøsyk.
yay är SHER-sewk.

257. Please prepare my berth.
Vær så snill og gjør i stand køya mi.
vär saw snil aw yerr ee stahn KOY-ah mee.

258. I am going to my stateroom.
Jeg går til lugaren min.
yay gawr til lew-GAH-ren meen.

259. Will you close the porthole?
Vil De lukke koøyet?
vil dee LEWK-eh KOO-oy-eh?

260. Let's go to the dining room.
La oss gå til spisesalen.
lah awss gaw til SPEE-seh-sah-len.

261. Can I have breakfast in my cabin?
Kan jeg få frokost i lugaren min?
*kahn yay faw FROO-kawst ee lew-GAH-ren
meen?*

262. A lifeboat. A life preserver. A porthole
En livbåt. Et livbelte. Et koøye.
*en LEEV-BAWT. et LEEV-belt-eh. et
KOO-oy-eh.*

BUS

BUSS

263. Where is the bus station?
Hvor er busstasjonen?
VOOR är BEWSS-stah-shoon-en?

264. Can I buy an excursion ticket?
Kan jeg kjøpe en billett til utflukten?
*kahn yay CHĒR-peh en bee-LET til EWT-flewk-
ten?*

265. Shall we stop for lunch?
Skal vi stanse for lunsj?
skahl vee STAHN-seh fawr lērnsh?

266. May I stop on the way?
Kan jeg stanse på veien?
kahn yay STAHN-seh paw VAY-en?

AUTOMOBILE

BIL

267. Where is a gas station (garage)?
Hvor er en bensinstasjon (garasje)?
voor är en ben-SEEN-stah-SHOON (gah-RAH-sheh)?

268. Is the road good (paved)?
Er veien bra, (asfaltert)?.
är VAY-en BRAH (AHSS-fahl-TERT)?

269. What town is this (the next one)?
Hva for en by er dette (den neste)?
vah fawr en bew är DET-eh (den NEST-eh)?

270. Where does that road go?
Hvor går den veien?
VOOR gawr den VAY-en?

271. Can you show it to me on the map?
Kan De vise meg den på kartet?
kahn dee VEESS-eh may den paw KAHRT-eh?

272. The tourist club.
Turistklubben.
tew-REEST-clewb-en.

273. I have an international driver's license.
Jeg har et internasjonalt kjørekort.
yay hahr et IN-tehr-nah-shoo-nahlt CHER-reh-KOORT.

274. How much is gas a liter?
Hva koster bensinen pr. liter?
vah KAWST-eh ben-SEEN-en pär LEE-tehr?

275. Give me —— liters.
La meg få —— liter.
LAH may faw —— LEE-tehr.

276. Please change the oil.
Vær så snill og bytt olje.
vår saw snil aw BEWT-AWL-yeh.

277. Light (medium, heavy) oil.
Lett (middels, tung) olje.
let (MEED-elss, toong) AWL-yeh.

278. Put water in the battery.
Fyll vann på batteriet.
FEWL VAHN paw BAHT-teh-REE-eh.

279. Recharge the battery.
Lad opp batteriet igjen.
LAHD awp BAHT-teh-REE-eh ee-YEN.

280. Will you lubricate the car?
Vil De smøre bilen?
vil dee SMER-reh BEEL-en?

281. Could you wash it now (soon)?
Kan De vaske den nå (snart)?
kahn dee VAHSK-eh den naw (snahrt)?

282. Tighten the brakes.
Stram bremsene.
STRAHM BREMS-eh-neh.

283. Will you check the tires?
Vil De kontrollere bilringene?
vil dee kawn-TRAWL-eh-reh BEEL-ring-eh-neh?

284. Can you fix the flat tire?
Kan De reparere en punktering?
kahn dee REH-pah-REH-reh en pewnk-TEH-ring?

285. Can you recommend a good mechanic?
Kan De anbefale en god mekaniker?
kahn dee AHN-beh-FAHL-eh en goo meh-KAHN-eek-ehr?

286. I want some air.
Jeg vil ha litt luft.
yay vil hah lit LEWFT.

287. A puncture.
En punktering.
en pewnk-TEH-ring.

288. The brake does not work well.
Bremsen fungerer ikke bra.
BREM-sen fewng-GEH-rer IK-eh brah.

289. Can you give me a lift to ——?
Kan jeg få sitte på til ——?
kahn yay faw SIT-teh paw til ——?

290. Is anything wrong?
Er det noe i veien?
är deh NOO-eh ee VAY-en?

291. There is a grinding (leak, noise).
Det er en skrapning (lekkasje, støy).
deh är en SKRAHP-ning (lek-KAH-sheh, STOY).

292. The engine overheats.
Motoren er overvarm.
MOO-too-ren är AWV-ehr-VAHRM.

293. The engine misses (stalls).
Motoren tenner ikke (fusker).
MOO-too-ren TEN-ehr IK-eh (FEWSK-ehr).

294. May I park here for a while?
Kan jeg parkere her en stund?
KAHN yay pahr-KAY-reh HÄR en STEWN?

295. I want to garage my car for the night.
Jeg vil gjerne ha bilen i garasjen i natt.
YAY vil YÄR-neh hah BEEL-en ee gah-RAH-shen ee naht.

296. When does it open (close)?
Når åpner (lukker) den?
NAWR AWP-nehr (LEWK-ehr) den?

HELP ON THE ROAD

HJELP PÅ VEIEN

297. I am sorry to trouble you.
Jeg beklager å måtte bry Dem.
yay beh-KLAHG-er aw MAWT-eh BR̄EW dem.

298. My car has broken down.
Bilen min har gått i stykker.
BEEL-en meen hahr gawt ee ST̄EWK-ehr.

299. Can you tow me?
Kan De ta meg på slep?
kahn dee tah may paw shlep?

300. Can you give me a lift to ——?
Kan De la meg få sitte på til ——?
kahn dee lah may faw SIT-teh paw til ——?

301. Can you help me jack up the car?
Kan De hjelpe meg med å jekke opp bilen?
kahn dee YELP-eh may meh aw YEK-eh awp BEEL-en?

302. Will you help me put on the spare?
Kan De hjelpe meg med å sette på reserve-
hjulet?
kahn dee YELP-eh may meh aw SET-teh paw reh-
SÄRV-eh-YEWL-eh?

303. Could you give me some gas?
Kan De gi meg litt bensin?
kahn dee yee may lit ben-SEEN?

304. Will you take me to a garage?
Vil De ta meg med til en garasje?
vil dee tah may meh til en gah-RAH-sheh?

305. Will you help me get the car off the road?
Vil De hjelpe meg med å få bilen ut av veien?
vil dee YELP-eh may meh aw faw BEEL-en ewt
ahv VAY-en?

306. My car is stuck in the mud.
Bilen min sitter fast i sølen.
BEEL-en meen SIT-ehr fahst ee SĒRL-en.

307. It is in the ditch.
Den er i grøfta.
den är ee GRĒRF-tah.

ROAD SIGNS AND PUBLIC NOTICES
VEISKILT OG OFFENTLIGE OPPSLAG
This section has been alphabetized in Norwegian
to facilitate the tourists' reading of Norwegian signs.

308. Keep out.   Adgang forbudt.
AHD-gahng fawr-BEWT.

309. Danger.   Fare.   *FAH-reh.*

310. Entrance. Inngang. *IN-gahng.*

311. Detour. Omvei OR: Tilbake.
   OHM-vay OR: *til-BAH-keh.*

312. Public Notice. Oppslag. *AWP-shlahg.*

313. Parking. Parkering. *pahr-KEH-ring.*

314. No parking. Parkering forbudt.
   pahr-KEH-ring fawr-BEWT.

315. Slow down. Reduser farten.
   ray-DEW-sehr FAHRT-en.

316. No smoking. Røkning forbudt.
   RERK-ning fawr-BEWT.

317. Closed. Stengt. *stengt.*

318. Warning. Advarsel. *AHD-vahr-sel.*

319. Curve. Sving. *sving.*

320. Lavatory. Toalett OR: V.C.
   too-ah-LET OR: *VEH-SEH.*

321. Exit. Utgang. *EWT-gahng.*

322. Road repairs. Veiarbeid. *VAY-ahr-BAY.*

LOCAL BUS AND STREETCAR

LOKALBUSS OG SPORVOGN

323. The bus stop.
   Bussholdeplassen.
   BEWSS-hawl-eh-plahss-en.

324. The bus driver.
   Busskjøreren.
   BEWSS-cher-rehr-en.

325. What bus (streetcar) do I take?
Hvilken buss (sporvogn) skal jeg ta?
VEEL-ken bewss (SPOHR-vawgn) skah yay tah?

326. Where does the bus for —— stop?
Hvor stopper bussen til ——?
voor STAWP-ehr BEWSS-en til ——?

327. Do you go near —?
Kjører De nær ——?
CHĒR-rehr dee nær ——?

328. How much is the fare?
Hvor mye koster billetten?
voor MĒW-eh KAWST-ehr bee-LET-en?

329. A transfer, please.
En overgang, takk.
en aw-ver-GAHNG, tahk.

330. I want to get off at the next stop, please.
Jeg vil gå av på neste holdeplass.
*yay vil gaw ahv paw NEST-eh HAWL-eh-
PLAHSS.*

TAXI

DROSJE

331. Please call a taxi for me.
Vær så snill og bestill en drosje for meg.
văr saw snil aw beh-STIL en DRAW-sheh fawr may.

332. How far is it?
Hvor langt er det?
voor lahngt ăr deh?

333. How much will it cost?
Hvor mye koster det?
voor MĒW-eh KAWST-ehr deh?

334. That is too much.
Det er alt for mye.
deh är ahlt fawr MEW-eh.

335. What do you charge per hour (kilometre)?
Hvor mye tar De pr. time (kilometer)?
voor MEW-eh TAHR dee pär TEEM-eh (kyee-loo-meh-tehr)?

336. I just wish to drive around the city.
Jeg vil bare kjøre omkring i byen.
yay vil BAH-reh CHÖR-reh AWM-kring ee BEW-en.

337. Please drive more slowly (carefully).
Vær så snill og kjør langsomt (forsiktig).
vär saw snil aw CHÖRR LAHNG-sawmt (fawr-SHEEK-tee).

338. Stop here.
Stopp her.
stawp här.

339. Wait here for me.
Vent her på meg.
VENT här paw may.

340. How much do I owe you?
Hvor mye skylder jeg Dem?
voor MEW-eh SHEWL-ehr yay dem?

HOTEL

HOTELL

341. Which hotel is good (inexpensive)?
Hvilket hotell er bra (billig)?
VEEL-ket hoo-TEL är brah (BIL-lee)?

342. The best hotel?
Det beste hotellet?
deh BEST-eh hoo-TEL-eh?

343. Not too expensive.
Ikke for dyrt.
IK-eh fawr dewrt.

344. I (do not) want to be in the center of town.
Jeg vil (ikke) være midt i byen.
yay vil (IK-eh) VÅR-eh MIT ee BEW-en.

345 Where it is not noisy.
Hvor det ikke er støy.
voor deh IK-eh år stoy.

346. I have a reservation for ——.
Jeg har reservert for ——.
yay hahr reh-sär-VEHRT fawr ——.

347. I want to reserve a room.
Jeg vil bestille et rom.
yay vil beh-STIL-eh et ROOM.

348. I want a room with (without) meals.
Jeg vil ha et rom med (uten) måltider.
yay vil hah et ROOM meh (EWT-en) MAWL-tee-dehr.

349. I want a single room (double room).
Jeg vil ha et enkeltrum (dobbeltrom).
yay vil hah et ENK-elt-ROOM (DAWB-elt-ROOM).

350. A room with a double bed.
Et rom med dobbelseng.
et ROOM meh DAWB-el-seng.

351. Single bed.   Twin beds.
Enkelseng.   Dobbelseng.
ENK-el-seng.   DAWB-el-seng.

352. A suite.   With (bath, shower).
En suite.   Med (bad, dusj).
en SVEET.   meh (BAHD, DEWSH).

353. With a window (a balcony).
Med et vindu (en balkong).
meh et VEEN-dew (en bahl-KAWNG).

354. For —— days.   For tonight.
For —— dager.   For i natt.
fawr —— DAH-gehr.   fawr ee NAHT.

355. For —— persons.
For —— personer.
fawr —— payr-SOON-ehr.

356. What is the rate per day?
Hva koster det pr. dag?
vah KAWST-ehr deh păr dah?

357. Are tax and room service included?
Er skatt og servise inkludert?
är SKAHT aw SÄR-vee-seh in-klew-DEHRT?

358. A week.   A month.
Per uke?   Per måned?
păr EW-keh?   păr MAW-neh?

359. On what floor?
I hvilken etasje?
ee VEEL-ken eh-TAH-sheh?

360. Stairs.   Upstairs.   Downstairs.
Trapp.   Ovenpå.   Nedenunder.
trahp.   AWV-en-paw.   NAY-den-ewn-ehr.

361. Is there an elevator?
Fins det elevator?
fins deh eh-leh-VAH-toor?

362. Hot and cold water.
Varmt og kaldt vann.
vahrmt aw kahlt vahn.

363. Where is the bathroom?
Hvor er badet?
voor är BAHD-eh?

364. On a lower floor.   Higher up.
I en lavere etasje.   Høyere opp.
ee en LAH-vay-reh eh-TAH-sheh.   HOY-eh-reh awp.

365. Please register.
Vær så vennlig og skriv Dem inn i fremmed-
boka.
vär saw VEN-lee aw SKREEV dem in ee FRAYM-med-book-ah.

366. I should like to see the room.
Jeg vil gjerne se rommet.
yay vil YÄR-neh seh ROOM-eh.

367. I (do not) like this one.
Jeg liker (ikke) dette.
yay LEEK-ehr (IK-eh) DET-eh.

368. Have you something better?
Har De noe bedre?
hahr dee NOO-eh BEH-dreh?

369. Cheaper.   Larger.   Smaller.
Billigere.   Større.   Mindre.
BIL-lee-eh-reh.   STÄR-reh.   MEEN-dreh.

370. With more light.   More air.
Med mere lys.   Mere luft.
meh MEH-reh lewss.   MEH-reh LEWFT.

371. I want a room higher up.
Jeg vil ha et rom høyere opp.
yay vil hah et room HOY-eh-reh AWP.

372. I have baggage at the station.
Jeg har bagasje på stasjonen.
yay hahr bah-GAH-sheh paw stah-SHOON-en.

373. Will you send for my bags?
Vil De hente reiseveskene mine?
vil dee HEN-teh RAY-seh-vesk-eh-neh MEEN-eh?

374. Here is the check for my trunks.
Her er kvitteringen for koffertene mine.
hår år KVEET-eh-ring-en fawr KOOF-ehr-teh-neh MEEN-eh.

375. Please send bath towels to my room.
Vær så snill og send badehåndklær til værelset mitt.
vår saw snil aw sen BAHD-eh-HAWN-klår til VÅR-el-seh mit.

376. Washcloths.   Towels.
Vaskekluter.   Håndklær.
VAHSK-eh-klewt-ehr.   HAWN-klår.

377. Ice.   Ice water.   Ice Bucket.
Is.   Isvann.   Vinkjøler.
eess.   EESS-vahn.   veen-CHÖR-lehr.

378. Messenger.   Chamber maid.
Portiér, *m.*   Værelsespike.
POORT-ee-år.   VÅR-els-es-peek-eh.

379. How much should I tip the maid?

Hvor mye skal jeg gi piken i drikkepenger?

voor $\overline{MEW}$-eh skahl yay yee PEEK-en ee DRIK-eh-peng-ehr?

380. Please call me at —— o'clock.

Vennligst vekk meg klokka ——.

VEN-leegst VEK may KLUK-ah ——.

381. I want breakfast in my room.

Jeg vil ha frokost på rommet mitt.

yay vil hah FROO-kawst paw ROOM-eh mit.

382. Could I have some laundry done?

Kan jeg få vasket noe tøy?

kahn yay faw VAHSK-et NOO-eh toy?

383. I want some things pressed.

Jeg vil ha noen saker presset.

yay vil hah NOO-en SAHK-ehr PRESS-et.

384. I should like to speak to the manager.

Jeg vil gjerne snakke med direktøren.

yay vil YÄR-neh SNUK-eh meh dee-rek-$\overline{TER}$-ren.

385. My room key, please.

Nøkkelen til rommet mitt, takk.

$\overline{NERK}$-el-en til ROOM-eh mit, TAHK.

386. Have I any letters or messages?

Er det noen brev eller beskjed for meg?

är deh NOO-en BREV EL-leh beh-SHEH fawr MAY?

387. Is the room furnished?

Er værelset møblert?

är VÄR-el-seh $\overline{mer}$-BLEHRT?

388. How much is it a month?
Hva koster det per måned?
vah KAWST-ehr deh pår MAW-neh?

389. Blankets. The silver. Dishes.
Tepper. Sølvtøy. Tallerkener.
TEP-ehr. SĒRL-toy. tah-LÄRK-eh-ner.

390. Do you know a good cook (maid)?
Vet De om en god kokke (pike)?
VAYT dee awm en goo KAWK-eh (PEEK-eh)?

391. Where can I rent a garage?
Hvor kan jeg leie en garasje?
voor kahn yay LAY-eh en gah-RAH-sheh?

RESTAURANT

RESTAURANT

392. Where is there a good restaurant?
Hvor fins det en god restaurang?
voor FINSS deh en goo ress-tew-RAHNG?

393. Breakfast. Lunch. Dinner.
Frokost. Lunsj. Middag.
FROO-kawst. lewnsh. MID-dah.

394. Supper. A Sandwich (open).
Supé OR: Aftens. Et smørbrød.
sew-PEH OR: AHF-tenss. et SMĒRR-brer.

395. At what time is dinner served?
Når serveres middag?
nawr sär-VÄR-ess MID-dah?

396. Can we lunch (dine) now?
Kan vi ha lunsj (middag) nå?
kahn vee hah LEWNSH (MID-dah) naw?

397. The waitress.   The waiter.
Serveringsdamen.   Kelneren.
sär-VÄR-ingss-DAHM-en.   KEL-neh-ren.

398. Waiter!   The headwaiter.
Kelner!   Hovmesteren.
KEL-ner!   HAWV-mest-eh-ren.

399. There are two (five) of us.   A cloakroom.
Vi er to (fem).   En garderobe.
vee är too.   en gahr-deh-ROO-beh.

400. Give me a table inside (outside, near the window).
Gi meg et bord innafor (utafor, nær vinduet).
yee may et boor IN-ah-fawr (EWT-ah-fawr, når veen-DEW-eh).

401. At the side.   In the corner.
På siden.   I hjørnet.
paw SEE-den.   ee YERR-neh.

402. Is this table reserved?
Er dette bordet opptatt?
är DET-eh BOOR-eh AWP-taht?

403. That one will be free soon.
Dette vil snart bli ledig.
DET-eh vil SNAHRT blee LEH-dee.

404. Where can I wash up?
Hvor kan jeg vaske meg?
voor kahn yay VAHSK-eh may?

405. Please serve us quickly.
Vennligst server oss fort.
VEN-leegst sär-VEHR awss FOORT.

406. We want to dine à la carte.
Vi vil spise middag à la carte.
vee vil SPEE-seh MID-dah ah lah kahrt.

407. Table d'hôte.
Dagens menu.
DAH-genss meh-N̄EW.

408. What is the specialty of the house?
Hva er restaurangens spesialiteter?
vah är reh-stew-RAHNG-enss speh-see-ah-lee-TEH-ter?

409. Bring me the menu (wine list).
Bring meg spisekortet (vinlisten), takk.
BRING may SPEE-seh-kawrt-eh (veen-LIST-en), tahk.

410. A plate.   A napkin.
En tallerken.   En serviett.
en tah-LÄRK-en.   en sehr-vee-ET.

411. A knife.   A fork.
En kniv.   En gaffel.
en KNEEV.   en GAHF-fel.

412. A large spoon.   A teaspoon.
En stor skje.   En teskje.
en STOOR sheh.   en TEH-sheh.

413. This is not clean.
Dette er ikke rent.
DET-eh är IK-eh RAYNT.

414. A (little) more of this, please.
(Litt) mere av dette, takk.
(LIT) MEH-reh ahv DET-eh, tahk.

415. I have had enough, thanks.
Takk, jeg er forsynt.
tahk, yay är fawr-SHEWNT.

416. I want something simple.
Jeg vil ha noe enkelt.
yay vil HAH NOO-eh ENK-elt.

417. Not too spicy.
Ikke for krydret.
IK-eh fawr KREWD-ret.

418. I like the meat cooked rare (well done, broiled, fried).
Jeg vil ha kjøttet lettstekt (velstekt, ovnstekt, stekt).
yay vil hah CHER-teh LET-stekt (VEL-stekt, AWN-stekt, stekt).

419. This is overcooked.
Dette er kokt for lenge.
DET-eh är kookt fawr LENG-eh.

420. This is undercooked.
Dette er kokt for lite.
DET-eh är kookt fawr LEET-eh.

421. This is too tough (sweet, sour).
Dette er for seigt (søtt, surt).
DET-eh är fawr SAYGT (SERT, SEWRT).

422. Rare. Well done.
Lettstekt. Gjennomstekt.
LET-stekt. YEN-awm-stekt.

423. This is cold.
Dette er kaldt.
DET-eh är KAHLT.

424. Take it away, please.
Vennligst ta det bort.
VEN-leegst TAH deh boort.

425. I did not order this.
Jeg bestilte ikke dette.
yay beh-STEEL-teh IK-eh DET-eh.

426. May I change this for ——?
Kan jeg bytte ut dette mot ——?
*kahn yay BEWT-eh ewt DET-eh MOOT
——?*

427. May I see your pastries?
Kan jeg få se kakene, takk?
kahn yay faw seh KAHK-eh-neh, tahk?

428. Ask the headwaiter to come here.
Be hovmesteren komme hit.
beh HAWV-mest-eh-ren KAWM-eh HEET.

429. The check, please.
Regningen, takk.
RAY-ning-en, TAHK.

430. Is the tip included?
Er drikkepenger iberegnet?
är DRIK-eh-päng-ehr ee-beh-RAY-net?

431. Is the service charge included?
Er servisen iberegnet?
är SÄR-vee-sen ee-beh-RAY-net?

432. What are these charges for?
Hva er det her for?
vah är deh här fawr?

433. There is a mistake in the bill.
Det er en feil på regningen.
deh är en FAYL paw RAY-ning-en.

434. Keep the change.
Behold vekslepengene.
beh-HAWL VEKS-leh-PENG-eh-neh.

435. Kindly pay at the cashier's.
Betal i kassen, takk.
beh-TAHL ee KAH-sen, tahk.

CAFÉ

KAFÉ

436. Bartender. Bartender, *c.*
BAHR-TEEN-der.

437. A cocktail. En cocktail. *en KAWK-tayl.*

438. An (alcoholic)drink. En drink. *en drink.*

439. Hard liquor. Brennevin, *c.*
BRAYN-neh-veen.

440. A liqueur. En likør. *en li-KERR.*

441. Fruit drink. Fruktsaft, *c.*
FREWKT-sahft.

442. A soft drink. Brus, *c.* *brewss.*

443. A small (large) bottle of ——.
En liten (stor) flaske med ——.
en LEE-ten (STOOR) FLAHSK-eh meh ——.

444. A glass of ——. Et glass ——.
et GLAHSS ——.

445. Draught beer. Fatøl. *FAHT-erl.*

446. Beer (light, dark). Øl (lyst, mørkt), *c.*
erl (lewst, mert).

447. Wine (red, white). Vin (rød, hvit), *c.*
veen (rer, veet).

448. Whiskey (and soda). Whisky (og soda).
VISS-key (aw SOO-dah).

449. Highball. Pjolter. *PYAWL-ter.*

450. Port. Portvin, *c.* *POORT-veen.*

451. Rum. Rom, *c.* *room.*

452. Claret. Rødvin, *c.* *RER-veen.*

453. Lemonade. Sitronbrus, *c.*
see-TROON-brewss.

454. Gin. Sjenever, *c.* *Sheh-NAY-ver.*

455. Cognac. Konjakk, *c.* *KAWN-yahk.*

456. Champagne. Champagne, *c.*
shahm-PAHN-yeh.

FOOD

MAT

*This section has been alphabetized in Norwegian to
facilitate the tourists' reading of Norwegian menus.*

FISH

FISK

457. Abbor, *c.* *AHB-boor.* **Perch.**

458. Aure, *c.* *OY-reh.* **Trout.**

459. Avkokt Torsk. *AHV-kookt TAWSHK.*
Boiled Cod.

460. Brisling, *c.* *BRISS-ling.* **Sprat.**

461. Fiskeboller. *FISS-keh-bawl-ehr.*
Fish balls.

462. Flyndre, *c.* *FLEWN-dreh.* **Flounder.**

463. Fiskekaker. *FISS-keh-kahk-ehr.* **Fish cakes.**

464. Fiskepudding, *c.* *FISS-keh-PEWD-deeng.*
Fish pudding.

465. Fiskegratin, *c.* *FISS-keh-grah-TAYNG.*
Fish soufflé.

466. Gjedde, *c.* *YAYD-eh.* **Pike.**

467. Hellefisk OR: Kveite, *c.* *HAYL-leh-fisk* OR:
KVAY-teh. **Halibut.**

468. Hummer, *c.* *HOOM-er.* **Lobster.**

469. Hvitting, *c.* *VIT-ting.* **Whiting.**

470. Karpe, *c.* *KAHR-peh.* **Carp.**

471. Kolje, *c.* *KAWL-yeh.* **Haddock.**

472. Krabbe, *c.* *KRAHB-eh.* **Crab.**

473. Kreps, *c.* *krayps.* **Crayfish.**

474. Laks, *c.* *lahks.* **Salmon.**

475. Lutefisk, *c.* *LEW-teh-fisk.*
Prepared from codfish in potash lye.

476. Reker. *RAY-ker.* **Shrimps.**

477. Rødspette, *c.* *RER-spayt-teh.* **Plaice.**

478. Røket laks, *c.* *RER-ket LAHKS.*
Smoked salmon.

479. Sardiner. *sahr-DEEN-er.* **Sardines.**

480. Sild, *c.*   *sil.*   **Herring.**

481. Spekesild, *c.*   *SPEK-eh-sil.*
Pickled Herring.

482. Tungeflyndre, *c.*   *TOONG-eh-FLEWN-dreh.*
Sole.

483. Ørret, *c.*   *ER-ret.*   **Trout.**

484. Østers.   *ERS-tayrss.*   **Oysters.**

485. Ål, *c.*   *awl.*   **Eel.**

MEATS AND FOWLS

KJØTT OG FUGL

486. Åkerhøne, *c.*   *AW-ker-her-neh.*   **Partridge.**

487. And, *c.*   *ahn.*   **Duck.**

488. Biff, *c.*   *bif.*   **Beefsteak.**

489. Chateaubriand, *c.*   *Shah-taw-bree-AHN.*
Chop of beef fillet.

490. Due, *c.*   *DEW-eh.*   **Pigeon.**

491. Fasan, *c.*   *fah-SAHN.*   **Pheasant.**

492. Flesk, *n.*   *flesk.*   **Pork.**

493. Fjærfe, *n.*   *FYÄR-feh.*   **Poultry.**

494. Fenalår, *n.*   *FEN-ah-LAWR.*
Cured, smoked leg of mutton.

495. Frikassé, *c.*   *free-kah-SAY.*   **Stew.**

496. Fylt kålhode, *n.*   *fewlt KAWL-hoh-deh.*
Stuffed cabbage.

497. Fårekjøtt, *n.*   *FAW-reh-CHERT.*   **Mutton.**

498. Fårekotelett, *m.* *FAW-reh-KAW-teh-let.*
Mutton chop.

499. Gås, *f.* *gawss.* **Goose.**

500. Hare, *m.* *HAHR-eh.* **Hare.**

501. Høne, *f.* *HER-neh.* **Hen, chicken.**

502. Hakket kjøtt, *n.* *HAHK-ket-CHERT.*
Chopped meat.

503. Kalkun, *c.* *kahl-KEWN.* **Turkey.**

504. Kalv, *c.* *kahlv.* **Veal.**

505. Kalvestek, *c.* *KAHLV-eh-stek.* **Roast veal.**

506. Kalvefilé, *c.* *KAHLV-eh-fee-LAY.*
Filet of veal.

507. Kokt skinke, *c.* *KOOKT SHEENK-eh.*
Boiled Ham.

508. Lapskaus, *c.* *LAHPSS-koyss.* **Hash.**

509. Kanin, *c.* *kah-NEEN.* **Rabbit.**

510. Kjøttretter. *CHERT-RAYT-ter.*
Meat dishes.

511. Kjøttboller, *c.* *CHERT-BAWL-ehr.*
Meat balls.

512. Kjøttkaker, *pl.* *CHERT-KAHK-ehr.*
Meat cakes ("Hamburgers").

513. Kjøttpålegg, *n.* *CHERT-paw-leg.* **Cold cuts**

514. Kotelett, *c.* *kaw-teh-LET.* **Chop, cutlet.**

515. Kylling, *c.* *CHEW-ling.* **Chicken.**

516. Lam, *n.* *lahm.* **Lamb.**

517. Lammestek, *c.* *LAHM-meh-stek.*
Roast leg of lamb.

518. Lammekotelett. *LAHM-meh-kaw-teh-LET.*
Lamb chop.

519. Lever, *c.* *LAY-ver.* **Liver.**

520. Matfett, *n.* *MAHT-fet.* **Lard.**

521. Medisterkaker, *c.* *meh-DISS-ter-kah-ker.*
Pork meat cakes

522. Nyrer, *pl.* $N\overline{EW}$-*rer.* **Kidneys.**

523. Oksekarbonade, *c.* OOK-*seh-kahr-boh-NAH-deh.*
Cakes of chopped beef.

524. Oksekjøtt, *n.* OOK-*say-chert.* **Beef.**

525. Oksestek, *c.* OOK-*say-stek.* **Roast leg of beef.**

526. Pølse, *c.* $P\overline{ERL}$-*seh.* **Sausage.**

527. Rapphøns, *c.* *RAHP-hernss.* **Partridge.**

528. Rensdyrstek. $RENSS$-*dewr-stek.*
Roast leg of reindeer (venison).

529. Rostbiff, *c.* *RAWST-biff.* **Roast beef.**

530. Saus, *c.* *sawss.* **Sauce.**

531. Skinke, *f.* *SHEENK-eh.* **Ham.**

532. Spekekjøtt, *n.* $SPAY$-*keh-CH$\overline{ERT}$.*
Dried mutton leg.

533. Sprengt, hermetisk kjøtt, *n.*
$SPR\ddot{A}NKT$, *här-MAY-tisk CH$\overline{ERT}$.*
Corned beef.

534. Stek, *c.* *stek.* **Roast.**

535. Svinekjøtt, *n.* *SVEE-neh-chert*. **Pork meat.**

536. Tunge, *c.* *TOONG-eh.* **Tongue.**

537. Varme pølser. *VAHR-meh PERL-ser*. **"Hot dogs," "Frankfurters."**

538. Wienerschnitzel, *c.* *VEE-nehr-SHNIT-sel*. **Veal filet steak.**

VEGETABLES

GRØNNSAKER

539. Agurker. *ah-GEWR-kahr*. **Cucumbers.**

540. Asparges. *ah-SPAHR-gess*. **Asparagus.**

541. Blomkål. *BLAWM-kawl*. **Cauliflower.**

542. Bønner. *BERN-ner*. **Beans.**

543. Erter. *ÄRT-er*. **Peas.**

544. Gresskar, *n.* *GRESS-kahr*. **Pumpkin.**

545. Grønnsaksuppe, *c.* *GRERN-sahk-sewp-eh*. **Vegetable soup.**

546. Gulrøtter. *GEWL-rert-ter*. **Carrots.**

547. Hvitløk, *c.* *VEET-lerk*. **Garlic.**

548. Hvitkål, *c.* *VEET-kawl*. **White cabbage.**

549. Kål, *c.* *kawl*. **Cabbage.**

550. Løk, *c.* *lerk*. **Onions.**

551. Mais, *c.* *MAH-ees*. **Corn.**

552. Neper, *c.* *NAY-pehr*. **Turnips.**

553. Olivener. *oo-LEE-veh-nehr*. **Olives.**

554. Persille, *c.* *per-SILL-eh.* **Parsley.**

555. Potetpuré, *c.* *poo-TAYT-pew-reh.*
Mashed potatoes.

556. Poteter (kokte, ovnstekte, stekte).
poo-TAYT-ehr (*KOOK-teh,* *AWN-stek-teh,*
STEK-teh).
Potatoes (boiled, baked, fried).

557. Pikkels. *PIK-elss.* **Pickles.**

558. Pepperrot, *c.* *PEP-ehr-root.* **Horse-radish.**

559. Reddik, *c.* *RAYD-deek.* **Radish.**

560. Ris, *c.* *reess.* **Rice.**

561. Rosenkål, *c.* *ROO-sen-kawl.*
Brussels sprouts.

562. Rødbeter. *RER-bay-tehr.* **Beetroot.**

563. Salat, *c.* *sah-LAHT.* **Salad (prepared)**
OR: **Lettuce.**

564. Salat og tomater.
sah-LAHT aw too-MAH-tehr.
Lettuce and tomatoes.

565. Surkål, *c.* *SEWR-kawl.* **Sauerkraut.**

566. Selleri, *n.* *sel-eh-REE.* **Celery.**

567. Snittbønner. *SNIT-ber-nehr.* **String beans.**

568. Sopp, *c.* *sawp.* **Mushroom.**

569. Spinat, *c.* *spee-NAHT.* **Spinach.**

BREAD, EGG, CHEESE, Etc.
BRØD, EGG, OST, o.s.v.

570. Bløtkake. *BLERT-kah-keh.* **Cream cake.**

571. Bacon og egg. *BAY-ken aw egg.*
Bacon and eggs.

572. Bolle, *f.* *BAWL-eh.* **Bun, muffin.**

573. Brød. *brer.* **Bread.**

574. Bygg, *n.* *bewg.* **Barley.**

575. Egg, *n.* (eggerøre). *egg (EGG-eh-RER-reh).*
Egg (scrambled).

576. Egg (forlorne). *egg (fawr-LAWR-neh).*
Egg (poached).

577. Egg (bløtkokt). *egg (BLERT-kookt).*
Egg (softboiled).

578. Egg (hårdkokt). *egg (HAWR-kookt).*
Egg (hardboiled).

579. Finbrød, *n.* *FEEN-brer.* **Rye bread.**

580. Flatbrød, *n.* *FLAHT-brer.*
Crisp, thin unleavened bread.

581. Gammelost, *c.* *GAHM-mel-OOST.*
Limburger.

582. Gjetost, *c.* *YAYT-oost.* **Goat cheese.**

583. Grovbrød, *n.* *GRAWV-brer.*
Pumperknickel bread.

584. Grøt, *c.* *grert.* **Hot cereal.**

585. Havregrøt, *c.* *HAHV-reh-grert.* **Oatmeal.**

586. Havremel, *n.* *HAHV-ray-mell.* **Oats.**

587. Horn, *n.* *hoorn.* **Crescent.**

588. Hvetemel, *n.* *VEH-teh-mel.* **Wheat.**

589. Hvetebrød, *n.* *VAY-ter-BRER.*
White bread.

590. Kake, *f.* *KAHK-eh.* **Cake.**

591. Kavring, *f.* *KAHV-ring.* **Hard biscuit.**

592. Kjeks, *c.* *kyeks.* **Biscuits, crackers.**

593. Knekkebrød, *n.* *KNAYK-keh-brer.*
Thin crisp rye bread.

594. Korn, *n.* *koorn.* **Grain.**

595. Krem, *c.* *krem.* **Cream.**

596. (Hård) kringle, *c.* (*hawr*) *KRING-leh.*
Pretzel.

597. Kromkake, *c.* *KROOM-kah-keh.*
Crisp cake; egg-roll.

598. Lefse, *c.* *LAYF-seh.* **Flat bannock.**

599. Mel, *n.* *mel.* **Flour.**

600. Nøkkelost, *c.* *NERK-kel-oost.*
Sharp cheddar cheese.

601. Nybakt brød, *n.* *NEW-bahkt BRER.*
Fresh bread.

602. En omelett. *en aw-meh-LET.* **An omelet.**

603. Primost, *c.* *PREEM-oost.* **Whey cheese.**

604. Ristet brød (uten smør).
REEST-et brer (EWT-en SMERR).
Toast (without butter).

605. Ristet brød (og fruktsjelé).
REEST-et brer (aw FREWKT-shay-LAY).
Toast and jelly.

606. Rug, *c.* *rewg.* **Rye.**

607. Rugbrød, *n.* *REWG-brer.* **Rye bread.**

608. Rømmegrøt, *c.*   *RĒRM-meh-GRĒRT.*
Cream pudding.

609. Rødgrøt, *c.*   *RĒR-grert.*   **Fruit pudding.**

610. Rundstykke, *n.*   *REWN-stewk-keh.*
Hard roll.

611. Skinke og egg.   *SHEENK-eh aw egg.*
Ham and eggs.

612. Smør, *n.*   *smērr.*   **Butter.**

613. Smørbrød, *n.*   *SMĒRR-brēr.*
Bread and butter OR: **open sandwich.**

614. Smørgåsbord, *n.*   *SMĒRR-gawss-BOOR.*
Hors d'œuvre.

615. Speilegg, *n.*   *SPAYL-egg.*   **Fried egg.**

616. Småkaker.   *SMAW-kahk-ehr.*   **Cookies.**

617. Sveitserost, *c.*   *SVAYT-sehr-OOST.*
Swiss cheese.

618. Tørre kaker.   *TĒR-reh KAHK-ehr.*   **Cookies.**

619. Vaniljepudding, *c.*
vah-NEEL-yah-PEWD-deeng.   **Custard.**

620. Wienerbrød, *n.*   *VEE-ner-BRĒR*
Danish pastry.

FRUITS, BERRIES AND NUTS

FRUKT, BÆR OG NØTTER

621. Ananas, *c.*   *AH-nah-nahs.*   **Pineapple.**

622. En appelsin.   *en ah-pel-SEEN.*   **An orange.**

623. Aprikos, *m.* *ah-pree-KOOS.* **Apricot.**

624. Artisjokk, *m.* *AHR-tee-shawk.* **Artichoke.**

625. Banan, *m.* *bah-NAHN.* **Banana.**

626. Bjørnebær, *n.* *BYER-neh-BÄR.*
Blackberries.

627. Blåbær, *n.* *BLAW-bär.* **Blueberries.**

628. Bringebær, *n.* *BREEN-gay-bär.* **Raspberry.**

629. Dadler. *DAHD-lehr.* **Dates.**

630. Druer. *DREW-er.* **Grapes.**

631. Eple, *n.* *AYP-leh.* **Apple.**

632. Eplekake, *m.* *EP-leh-kahk-eh.*
Apple pie.

633. Fersken, *m.* *FÄRSH-ken.* **Peach.**

634. Fiken, *c.* *FEE-ken.* **Fig.**

635. Fruktkompott, *c.* *FREWKT-kawm-pawt.*
Stewed and mixed fruit.

636. Grapefrukt, *c.* *GRAYP-frewkt.* **Grapefruit.**

637. Hasselnøtter. *HAHSS-el-nert-ehr.*
Hazelnuts.

638. Jordbær, *n.* *YOOR-bär.* **Strawberries.**

639. Jordnøtter. *YOOR-nert-ehr.* **Peanuts.**

640. Kastanjer. *kah-STAHN-yeh.* **Chestnuts.**

641. Kirsebær, *n.* *CHEER-seh-bär.* **Cherries.**

642. Mandler. *MAHND-lehr.* **Almonds.**

643. Melon, *c.* *MAY-loon.* **Melon.**

644. Multer. *MEWL-tehr*. **Cloudberries.**

645. Nyper. $\overline{NEW}$-*pehr*. **Hips.**

646. Plommer. *PLAWM-ehr*. **Plums.**

647. Pærer. *PĂR-ehr*. **Pears.**

648. Rabarbra, *c.* *rah-BAHR-brah*. **Rhubarb.**

649. Rips, *c.* *reeps*. **(Red) Currants.**

650. Rosin, *c.* *roo-SEEN*. **Raisin.**

651. Sitron, *c.* *see-TROON*. **Lemon.**

652. Sjelé, *c.* *shay-LAY*. **Jelly.**

653. Solbær, *n.* *SOOL-băr*. **Black currants.**

654. Stikkelsbær, *n.* *STEEK-els-băr*.
Gooseberries.

655. Svisker. *SVISK-ehr*. **Prunes.**

656. Tranebær, *n.* *TRAHN-eh-băr*. **Cranberry.**

657. Tyttebær, *n.* $T\overline{EW}T$-*eh-băr*.
Red whortleberries.

658. Valnøtter. *VAHL-$\overline{ne}$rt-ehr*. **Walnuts.**

659. Vannmelon, *c.* *VAHN-meh-loon*.
Watermelon.

BEVERAGES

VARERDRIKKE

660. Appelsinsaft, *c.* *ah-pel-SEEN-sahft*.
Orange juice.

661. Fløte, *c.* *FLĒR-teh*. **Cream.**

662. Fruktsaft, *c.* *FROOKT-sahft.* **Fruit juice.**

663. Kaffe, *c.* *KAHF-feh.* **Coffee.**

664. Kakao, *c.* *kah-KAH-oo.* **Cocoa.**

665. Limonade, *c.* *lee-moo-NAH-deh.*
Lemonade.

666. Mineralvann, *n.* *mee-neh-rahl-VAHN.*
Mineral water.

667. Melk (nysilt, skummet, sur), *c.*
melk (*NEW-seelt, SKOOM-et, sewr*).
Milk (fresh, skimmed, sour).

668. Sjokolade, *c.* *SHOO-koo-LAH-deh.*
Chocolate.

669. Tomatsaft, *c.* *too-MAHT-sahft.*
Tomato juice.

670. Te, *c.* *teh.* **Tea.**

GROCERIES

KOLONIALVARER

671. Eddik, *c.* *AY-deek.* **Vinegar.**

672. Farin, *c.* *fah-REEN.* **Granulated sugar.**

673. Fruktsjelé, *c.* *frewkt-shay-LAY.* **Jelly.**

674. Hermetikk, *c.* *hår-meh-TEEK.*
Canned goods.

675. Ingefær, *c.* *EENG-eh-får.* **Ginger.**

676. Kolonialvarer. *koo-loo-nee-AHL-vahr-ehr.*
Groceries.

677. Krydderier. *KREWD-eh-REE-ehr.* **Spices.**

678. Majones, *c.* *mah-yoo-NAYSS.* **Mayonnaise.**

679. Olje, *c.* *AWL-yeh.* **Oil.**

680. Pepper, *c.* *PEP-ehr.* **Pepper.**

681. Salt, *n.* *sahlt.* **Salt.**

682. Sennep, *c.* *SEN-nep.* **Mustard.**

683. Sjelé, *c.* *shay-LAY.* **Jelly.**

684. Smult, *n.* *smewlt.* **Lard.**

685. Sukker, *n.* *SEWK-ehr.* **Sugar.**

686. Syltetøy, *n.* *SEWL-teh-toy.* **Jam.**

PLACES OF WORSHIP

KIRKER: SYNAGOGE

687. Where is there a service in English?
Hvor er det gudstjeneste på engelsk?
voor är deh GEWSS-chen-est-eh paw ENG-elsk?

688. A Catholic church.
En katolsk kirke.
en KAH-toolsk CHEER-keh.

689. A Protestant church.
En protestantisk kirke.
en proo-teh-STAHN-teesk CHEER-keh.

690. A synagogue.
En synagoge.
en SEW-nah-GOO-geh.

691. When is the service (mass)?
Når er gudstjenesten (messen)?
nawr är GEWSS-chen-est-en (MESS-en)?

692. Is there an English-speaking priest (rabbi minister)?

Fins det en engelsktalende pastor (rabbiner, prest)?

finss deh en ENG-elsk-TAHL-en-eh PAHSS-toor (RAH-bee-nehr, prest)?

693. Congregation. A sermon.

En menighet. En preken.

en MEN-ee-het. en PREH-ken.

SIGHTSEEING

SEVERDIGHETER

694. I want to hire a car.

Jeg vil leie en bil.

yay vil LAY-eh en BEEL.

695. I want a guide who speaks English.

Jeg vil ha en tolk som kan snakke engelsk.

yay vil hah en TAWLK sawm kahn SNUK-keh ENG-elsk.

696. Call for me tomorrow at my hotel at 9 o'clock.

Hent meg i morgen klokka 9 på hotellet.

hent may ee-MAWRN KLUK-ah nee paw hoo-TEL-eh.

697. What is the charge per hour (day)?

Hva koster det per time (dag)?

vah KAWST-eh deh păr TEEM-eh (dahg)?

698. How much do you want for the whole trip?

Hva tar De for hele turen?

vah TAHR dee fawr HAYL-eh TEW-ren?

699. Please show me all the sights of interest.

Vis meg alle severdigheter, er De snill.

VEESS may AHL-eh seh-VÄR-dee-HAY-tehr, är dee snil.

700. I am interested in archeology.

Jeg er interessert i arkeologi.

yay är in-teh-reh-SEHRT ee AHR-keh-oo-LOO-gee.

701. Scientist.

En vitenskapsmann.

en VEE-ten-SKAHPS-mahn.

702. (Art) Painter.   A Sculptor.

Kunstmaler, *c.*   Billedhogger, *c.*

KEWNST-mahl-ehr.   BEE-led-HAWG-ehr.

703. Applied Art.

Kunstindustri.

KEWNST-een-dew-stree.

704. Native arts and crafts.

Kunsthåndverk og hjemmeindustri.

KEWNST-hawnd-VÄRK aw YEM-meh-een-dew-stree.

705. Painting.   Sculpture.

Malerier.   Skulpturer.

mahl-eh-REE-ehr.   skewlp-TEWR-ehr.

706. Ruins.   Architecture.

Ruiner.   Arkitektur.

rew-EE-nehr.   ahr-kee-TEK-tewr.

707. Shall I have time to visit the museum?

Får jeg tid til å besøke museet?

fawr yay TEE til aw beh-SÖRK-ehr mew-SEH-eh?

708. How long does it take to walk?
Hvor langt er det å gå?
voor LAHNGT är deh aw gaw?

709. The cathedral. The monastery.
Domkirken. Klosteret.
DAWM-cheer-ken. KLAWST-eh-reh.

710. The castle. The museum.
Borgen. Museet.
BAWR-gen. mew-SEH-eh.

711. Is it (still) open?
Er det (framleis) åpent?
är deh (FRAHM-layss) AWP-ent?

712. How long does it stay open?
Hvor lenge er det åpent?
voor LENG-eh är deh AWP-ent?

713. We want to stop for refreshments.
Vi vil stanse og ha forfriskninger.
vee vil STAHN-seh aw hah fawr-FREESK-ning-ehr.

714. How long must I wait?
Hvor lenge må jeg vente?
voor LENG-eh maw yay VENT-eh?

715. Where is the entrance (the exit)?
Hvor er inngangen (utgangen)?
voor är IN-gahng-en (EWT-gahng-en)?

716. What is the price of admission?
Hva koster det å komme inn?
vah KAWST-ehr deh aw KAWM-eh in?

717. Do we need an interpreter?
Trenger vi en tolk?
TRENG-er vee en TAWLK?

718. How much is the guidebook?
Hva koster reisehåndboka?
vah KAWST-ehr RAY-seh-hawn-BOOK-ah?

719. May I take photographs?
Får jeg ta fotografier?
fawr yay tah foo-too-grah-FEE-er?

720. We want to stop for postcards (souvenirs).
Vi vil stanse for brevkort (souvenirer).
Vee vil STAHN-seh fawr BRAYV-koort (SEW-vay-neer-ehr).

721. Do you have a book in English about ——?
Har De en bok på engelsk om ——?
hahr dee en book paw ENG-elsk awm ——?

722. Drive me back to the hotel.
Kjør meg tilbake til hotellet.
CHERR may til-BAH-keh til hoo-TEL-eh.

723. Go back by way of the business section.
Kjør meg tilbake gjennom forretningsstrøket.
CHERR may til-BAH-keh YEN-oom fawr-RET-nings-strer-keh.

AMUSEMENTS

FORNØYELSER

724. The balcony.   Balkongen.
bahl-KAWNG-en.

725. The ballet.   Balleten.   *BAH-let-en.*

726. The beach.   Stranden.   *STRAHN-en.*

727. The box.   Losjen.   *LOO-shen.*

728. The box office. Billettluken.
bee-LET-lewk-en.

729. The café. Kaféen. *kah-FAY-en.*

730. Concert. Konserten. *kawn-SÄRT-en.*

731. The cover charge. Servise, *c.*
sär-VEE-seh.

732. Fishing. Fiske. *FISS-keh.*

733. Folk dances. Folkedanser.
FAWK-eh-dahn-sehr.

734. Football field. En fotballbane.
en foot-bahl-BAHN-eh.

735. Gambling casino. Kasino, *c.*
kah-SEE-noo.

736. Golf. Golf, *c. gawlf.*

737. Golf clubs. Golfkøller. *GAWLF-kerl-ehr.*

738. Horse racing. Hesteveddeløp, *n.*
HEST-eh-ved-deh-LERP.

739. Minimum. Minimum. *MEE-nee-mewm.*

740. Movies. Kino, *c. CHEE-noo.*

741. Night club. Nattklubb, *c. NAHT-klewb.*

742. Opera. Opera, *c. OO-peh-rah.*

743. Opera glasses. Teaterkikkert, *c.*
teh-AHT-ehr-CHEEK-ehrt.

744. Orchestra seat. Første parkett, *n.*
fersh-teh pahr-KET.

745. A program. Et program. *et proo-GRAHM.*

746. Record. En grammofonplate.
en grah-moh-FOON-plah-teh.

747. A reserved seat. En reservert plass.
en reh-SÄR-vehrt PLAHSS.

748. A skater. En skøyteløper.
en SHOY-teh-LER-pehr.

749. Skating. Gå på skøyter.
gaw paw SHOY-tehr.

750. Skating rink. Skøytebane, *c.*
SHOY-teh-BAHN-eh.

751. A skating meet. Et skøyteløp.
et SHOY-teh-LERP.

752. Cross country skiing. Et langrenn.
et LAHNG-ren.

753. Ski poles. Skistaver. *SHEE-stahv-ehr.*

754. A ski meet. Et skirenn. *et SHEE-ren.*

755. A skier. En skiløper. *en SHEE-LER-pehr.*

756. Ski straps. Skibindinger.
SHEE-been-ing-ehr.

757. Swimming. Svømming. *SVERM-ming.*

758. Sled. En kjelke. *en CHEL-keh.*

759. Soccer. Fotball, *c.* *FOOT-bahl.*

760. Tennis. Tennis, *n.* *TEN-iss.*

761. Theater. Et teater. *et teh-AHT-ehr.*

762. Where can we go to dance?
Hvor kan vi gå å danse?
voor kahn vee gaw aw DAHN-seh?

763. May I have this dance?
Kan jeg få denne dansen?
kahn yay faw DEN-eh DAHN-sen?

764. Is there a matinee today?
Er det matiné i dag?
är deh MAH-tee-NEH ee-DAH?

765. When does the evening performance start?
Når begynner aftenforestillingen?
nawr beh-YEWN-ehr AHF-ten-fawr-eh-stil-ing-en?

766. Can you please play a foxtrot (rumba, tango, waltz)?
Vær så vennlig å spille en foxtrott (rumba, tango, vals).
vär saw VEN-lee aw SPIL-eh en FAWKS-trawt (REWM-bah, TAHNG-oo, vahlss).

767. Have you any seats for tonight?
Har De noen billetter for i kveld?
hahr dee NOO-en bee-LET-ehr fawr ee KVEL?

768. Can I see (hear) well from there?
Kan jeg se (høre) bra derfra?
kahn yay seh (HER-reh) brah DÄR-frah?

769. Not too near (far).
Ikke altfor nær (langt borte).
IK-eh AHLT-fawr NÄR (LAHNGT BOOR-teh).

770. The music is excellent.
Musikken er utmerket.
mew-SIK-en är EWT-mär-ket.

771. This is very interesting (funny).
Dette er meget interessant (morsomt).
DET-eh är MEH-get in-teh-reh-SAHNT
(*MOOR-shawmt*).

772. Is this intermission?
Er dette mellomakt?
är DET-eh MAYL-oom-AHKT?

SHOPPING

I BUTIKKER

773. I want to go shopping.
Jeg vil gå å handle (OR: gå i butikker; gjøre innkjøp).
yay vil gaw aw HAHND-leh (OR: *gaw ee BEW-tik-ehr; YER-reh in-CHERP*).

774. Please drive me around the shopping center.
Vær så snill og kjør meg rundt i forretnings-strøket.
vär saw snil aw CHERR may rewnt ee fawr-RET-nings-STRER-keh.

775. I am just looking around.
Jeg bare ser meg om.
yay BAH-reh SAYR may awm.

776. May I speak to a salesman (salesgirl)?
Kan jeg få snakke med ekspeditøren (ekspeditrisen; OR: butikkdamen)?
kahn yay faw SNUK-keh meh eks-peh-dee-TER-ren (eks-peh-dee-TREE-sen, OR: bew-TIK-dahm-en)?

777. Is there an English-speaking person here?
Snakker noen engelsk her?
SNUK-er NOO-en ENG-elsk HÅR?

778. Where is the bakery (pastry) shop?
Hvor er bakeriet (konditoriet)?
voor år BAH-keh-REE-eh (koon-dee-too-REE-eh)?

779. An antique shop. Antikvitetshandel, *c.*
ahn-tee-kvee-TETS-HAHN-del.

780. A bookshop. En bokhandel.
en BOOK-hahn-del.

781. Butcher store. Slakterbutikk, *c.*
en SHLAHK-tehr-bew-TIK.

782. Candy store. Sjokoladeforretning, *c.*
SHOO-koo-LAH-deh-fawr-RET-ning.

783. Cigar store. Tobakksforretning, *c.*
too-BAHKS-fawr-RET-ning.

784. Clothing store. Kledehandel, *c.*
KLED-eh-HAHN-del.

785. A counter. En disk, *c. en disk.*

786. A department store.
Et varehus (OR: stormagasin).
et VAH-reh-hews (OR: STOOR-mah-gah-seen).

787. Dressmaker. Dameskredder, *c.*
DAHM-eh-skred-ehr.

788. Dry goods. Manufakturvarer.
mah-new-fahk-TEWR-vahr-ehr.

789. A drugstore. Et apotek.
et ah-poo-TEK.

790. Furrier. Pelsvarehandler, *c.*
PELSS-vah-reh-HAHN-lehr.

791. A grocery. En kolonialforretning.
en koh-loh-nee-AHL-fawr-RET-ning.

792. Hardware store. En jernvarehandler.
en YÆRN-vah-reh-HAHN-lehr.

793. Hat shop. En hatteforretning.
en HAHT-teh-fawr-RET-ning.

794. Jewelry. En gullsmed. *en GEWL-smeh.*

795. Manufacturer. En fabrikant.
en fah-bree-KAHNT.

796. Meat market. En kjøttforretning.
en CHERT-fawr-RET-ning.

797. Milliner. Motehandler, *c.*
MOO-teh-HAHN-lehr.

798. Shoe store. Skoforretning, *c.*
SKOO-fawr-RET-ning.

799. Shoemaker. En skomaker.
en SKOO-mahk-ehr.

800. Tailor shop. En skredderforretning.
en SKRED-ehr-fawr-RET-ning.

801. Toy shop. En leketøysbutikk.
en LEK-eh-toyss-bew-TIK.

802. Upholsterer. En salmaker.
en SAHL-mahk-ehr.

803. Watchmaker. En urmaker.
en EWR-mahk-ehr.

804. Please regulate my watch for me.
Vær så snill og reguler klokka for meg.
văr saw snil aw reh-gew-LEHR KLUK-ah fawr may.

805. How much will it cost to have it repaired?
Hva koster det å få den reparert?
vah KAWST-ehr deh aw faw den reh-pah-REHRT?

806. A sale.   Bargain sale.
Et salg.   Utsalg OR: Billigsalg.
et sahlg.   EWT-sahlg OR: BEE-lee-SAHLG.

807. I (I do not) like that.
Jeg liker (ikke) dette her.
yay LEEK-ehr (IK-eh) DET-eh hăr.

808. I want to buy ——.
Jeg ønsker å kjøpe ——.
yay ERN-skehr aw CHERP-eh ——.

809. How much is it (for each piece) all together?
Hvor mye koster det (for hvert stykke) tilsammen?
voor MEW-eh KAWST-ehr deh (fawr VĂRT STEWK-eh) til-SAHM-en?

810. It is very (much too) expensive.
Det er meget (altfor)dyrt.
deh ăr MEH-get (ahlt-fawr)DEWRT.

811. You said it would cost ——.
De sa det ville koste ——.
dee sah deh VIL-eh KAWST-eh ——.

812. I prefer something better (cheaper).
Jeg foretrekker noe bedre (billigere).
yay FAWR-eh-TRĂK-ehr NOO-eh BEH-dreh (BEE-lee-eh-reh).

813. Finer.   Finere.   *FEEN-eh-reh.*

814. Stronger.   Sterkere.   *STÄRK-eh-reh.*

815. Larger.   Større.   *STĒR-reh.*

816. Smaller.   Mindre.   *MIN-dreh.*

817. Longer.   Lengere.   *LENG-eh-reh.*

818. Shorter.   Kortere.   *KAWRT-eh-reh.*

819. Wider.   Videre.   *VEE-eh-reh.*

820. Narrower.   Trangere.   *TRAHNG-eh-reh.*

821. Heavier.   Tyngre.   *TĒWNG-reh.*

822. Thinner.   Tynnere.   *TĒWN-eh-reh.*

823. Thicker.   Tykkere.   *TĒWK-eh-reh.*

824. Lighter.   Lettere.   *LET-eh-reh.*

825. Tighter.   Tettere.   *TET-eh-reh.*

826. Looser.   Løsere.   *LĒRSS-eh-reh.*

827. Show me some others.
Vis meg noen andre.
veess may NOO-en AHN-dreh.

828. May I try this on?
Kan jeg prøve denne her?
kahn yay PRĒR-veh DEN-eh hãr?

829. Can I order one?
Kan jeg bestille denne?
kahn yay beh-STIL-eh DEN-eh?

830. When shall I call for it?
Når kan jeg hente den?
NAWR kahn yay HENT-eh den?

831. How long will it take?
Hvor lang tid vil det ta?
voor LAHNG tee vil deh tah?

832. Can you have it ready for this evening?
Kan De ha den ferdig i kveld?
kahn dee hah den FÆR-ee ee KVEL?

833. Please take my measurements.
Vær så vennlig å ta mål av meg.
vår saw VEN-lee aw tah MAWL ahv may.

834. It does not fit me.
Den passer meg ikke.
den PAHSS-ehr may IK-eh.

835. It is (not) becoming to me.
Den klær meg (ikke).
den KLÅR may (IK-eh).

836. Will this fade (shrink)?
Vil dette falme (krympe)? ___
vil DET-eh FAHL-meh (KREWM-peh)?

837. Will you wrap this please?
Vær så snill å pakke dette inn.
vår saw snil aw PAHK-eh DET-eh in.

838. I will take it with me.
Jeg vil ta det med meg.
yay vil TAH deh meh may.

839. Can you ship it to me freight?
Kan De sende det til meg som gods?
kahn dee SEN-eh deh til may sawm GOOSS?

840. Whom do I pay?
Hvem skal jeg betale?
vem skah yay beh-TAHL-eh?

841. Please bill me.
Vær så snill og send regning.
vår saw snil aw SEN RAY-ning.

842. Are there any other charges (delivery charges)?
Er det andre utgifter (leveringsavgift)?
år deh AHN-dreh EWT-yif-ter (LAY-veh-rings-ahv-YIFT)?

843. Let me have a sales slip.
La meg få kvittering.
LAH may faw kvee-TEH-ring.

844. You will be paid on delivery.
De vil bli betalt ved avleveringen.
dee vil blee beh-TAHLT veh AHV-leh-veh-ring-en.

845. Handle with care! This parcel is fragile (perishable).
Vær forsiktig! Denne pakken går lett i stykker (tar lett skade).
vår fawr-SHEEK-tee! DEN-eh PAHK-en gawr LET ee STEWK-ehr (TAHR let SKAH-deh).

846. Pack this carefully for export.
Pakk denne forsiktig for eksport, takk.
PAHK DEN-eh fawr-SHEEK-tee fawr EKS-poort, TAHK.

POST OFFICE

POSTKONTOR

847. Where is the post office?
Hvor er postkontoret?
voor år PAWST-koon-TOO-reh?

848. To which window do I go?
Hvilken luke skal jeg gå til?
VEEL-ken LEWK-eh skah yay gaw til?

849. A postcard. Et brevkort.
et BRAYV-koort.

850. A letter. Et brev. *et BRAYV.*

851. By airmail. Med flypost.
meh FLEW-pawst.

852. Parcel post. Pakkepost, *m.*
PAHK-eh-pawst.

853. Registered. Rekommandert.
reh-koo-mahn-DEHRT.

854. Insured. Forsikret. *fawr-SHEEK-ret.*

855. General Delivery. Poste Restante.
PAWST-eh reh-STAHN-teh.

856. Special delivery. Ekspress. *eks-PRESS.*

857. Samples, no value. Prøver uten verdi.
PRER-vehr EWT-en VÄR-dee.

858. Printed matter. Trykksaker.
TREWK-sahk-ehr.

859. A stamp. Et frimerke. *et FREE-mär-keh.*

860. Postage. Porto, *m.* *POOR-too.*

861. Cash on delivery. Postoppkrav, *n.*
PAWST-awp-krahv.

862. Cash discount. Kontantrabatt, *c.*
koon-TAHNT-rah-BAHT.

863. "To await arrival." "Hold til ankomst."
HAWL til AHN-kawmst.

864. Please forward. Bes ettersendt.
BEH-ess ET-ter-sent.

865. Three stamps of —— denomination.
Tre —— øres frimerker.
TREH —— ĒR-ress FREE-mär-kehr.

866. I want to send a money order.
Jeg vil sende en postanvisning.
yay vil SEN-eh en PAWST-ahn-VEESS-ning.

867. There is nothing dutiable on this.
Det er ingen toll på denne her.
deh är EENG-en TAWL paw DEN-eh här.

868. Will this go out today?
Går det her ut i dag?
GAWR deh här EWT ee-DAH?

869. Give me a receipt, please.
Vennligst gi meg en kvittering.
VEN-leegst yee may en kvee-TEH-ring.

BANK

BANK

870. Where is the nearest bank?
Hvor er den nærmeste banken?
voor är den NÄR-mest-eh BAHNK-en?

871. I want to send fifty dollars to the U.S.
Jeg vil sende femti dollar til De Forente
Stater.
*yay vil SEN-eh FEM-tee DAWL-ahr til dee
fawr-ENT-eh̦ STAHT-ehr.*

872. At which window can I change this?
I hvilken luke kan jeg veksle denne?
ee VEEL-ken LEWK-eh kahn yay VEKS-leh DEN-eh?

873. Will you cash a check?
Kan De løse inn en sjekk?
kahn dee LER-seh in en CHEK?

874. Fill in the forms.
Fyll ut blankettene.
FEWL ewt blahn-KET-eh-neh.

875. Can you change this for me?
Kan De veksle denne her for meg?
kahn dee VEKS-leh DEN-eh hăr fawr may?

876. Give me (do not give me) large bills.
Gi meg (ikke) store sedler.
yee may (IK-eh) STOO-reh SED-lehr.

877. May I have some change?
Kan jeg få småpenger?
kahn yay faw SMAW-peng-ehr?

878. I have traveler's checks.
Jeg har reisesjekker.
yay hahr RAY-seh-CHEK-ehr.

879. What is the exchange rate on the dollar?
Hva er kursen på dollar?
vah ăr KEW-shen paw DAWL-ahr?

880. A letter of credit.
Et reiseakkreditiv.
et RAY-seh-ah-kreh-dee-TEEV.

881. Deposit.   Quotation.
   Sette inn (OR: Deponere).   Kursnotering, *c.*
   SET-teh in (OR: *deh-poh-NAY-reh*).
   KEWRSS-noo-TEH-ring.

882. A bank draft.   Signature.
   En veksel.   Underskrift, *c.*
   en VEK-sel.   EWN-ehr-skrift.

BOOKSTORE AND STATIONER'S

BOK OG PAPIRHANDEL

883. Where is there a bookshop?
   Hvor er det en bokhandel?
   voor är deh en BOOK-hahn-del?

884. Can you recommend a book about ——?
   Kan De anbefale en bok om ——?
   kahn dee AHN-beh-FAHL-eh en book awm ——?

885. I want a map of ——.
   Jeg ønsker et kart over ——.
   yay ERN-skehr et KAHRT AW-vehr ——.

886. A stationer's.   En papirhandel.
   en pah-PEER-hahn-del.

887. A newsstand.   En kiosk.   *en kee-OHSK.*

888. Artist's material.   Kunstnermaterialer.
   KEWNST-nehr-mah-teh-REE-ahl-ehr.

889. A book.   En bok.   *en BOOK.*

890. Ball-point pen.   Kulepenn, *m.*
   KEWL-eh-pen.

891. A blotter.   Et trekkpapir.
   et TREK-pah-PEER.

892. A carbon paper. Et blåpapir.
et BLAW-pah-PEER.

893. Dictionary. En ordbok. *en OOR-book.*

894. Envelopes (airmail).
Konvolutter (flypost).
kawn-feh-LEWT-ehr (FLEW-pawst).

895. An eraser. Et viskelær. *et VISK-eh-lăr.*

896. Fountain pen. En fyllepenn.
en FEWL-eh-pen.

897. Guidebook. En "reisefører."
en RAY-seh-FER-rehr.

898. Ink. Blekk, *n.* *blek.*

899. Magazines. Tidsskrifter. *TISS-skrift-ehr.*

900. Newspapers. Aviser. *ah-VEESS-ehr.*

901. A pencil. En blyant. *en BLEW-ahnt.*

902. Playing cards. Spillkort. *SPIL-kawrt.*

903. Picture postcard. Et prospektkort.
et praw-SPEKT-kawrt.

904. Postcards. Brevkort, *n.* *BREV-koort.*

905. Publisher. En forlegger. *en FAWR-leg-ehr.*

906. Publishing company. Et forlag.
et FAWR-lahg.

907. Scotch tape. Gummiremser.
GOO-mee-REM-sehr.

908. A string. En hyssing. *en HEW-sing.*

909. Tissue paper. Silkepapir, *n.*
SIL-keh-pah-PEER.

910. Typewriter ribbon.
Fargeband for skrivemaskin.
FAHR-geh-bahn fawr SKREE-veh-mah-SHEEN.

911. Weeklies. Ukeblar. *EW-keh-BLAHR.*

912. Wrapping paper. Innpakningspapir.
IN-pahk-nings-pah-PEER.

913. Writing paper. Skrivepapir.
SKREE-veh-pah-PEER.

CIGAR STORE

SIGARBUTIKK

914. Where is the nearest cigar store?
Hvor er den nærmeste sigarbutikken?
voor år den NÅR-mest-eh si-GAHR-bew-TIK-en?

915. I want some cigars.
Jeg vil ha noen sigarer.
yay vil hah NOO-en si-GAHR-ehr.

916. A pack of American cigarettes, please.
En pakke amerikanske sigaretter, takk.
en PAHK-eh ah-meh-ree-KAHN-skeh si-gah-RET-ehr, TAHK.

917. Please show me some cigarette cases.
Vennligst vis meg noen sigarettetuier.
VEN-leegst VEESS may NOO-en si-gah-RET-eh-tew-ee-ehr.

918. I need a lighter.
Jeg trenger en sigarettenner.
yay TRENG-ehr en si-gah-RET-ten-ehr.

919. May I have a match, please?
Kan jeg få en fyrstikk, takk?
kahn yay faw en FEWR-stik, TAHK?

920. Flint. Flintstein, *m.* *FLINT-stayn.*

921. Matches. Fyrstikker. *FEWR-stik-ehr.*

922. A pipe. En pipe (OR: En snadde).
en PEEP-eh (OR: *en SNAHD-eh*).

923. Pipe tobacco. Pipetobakk, *c.*
PEEP-eh-too-BAHK.

924. A pouch. En tobakkspung.
en too-BAHKSS-poong.

925. Lighter fluid. Bensin, *m.* *ben-SEEN.*

BARBER SHOP AND BEAUTY PARLOR

BARBER- OG FRISØRSALONG

926. Where is there a good barber?
Hvor fins det en dyktig barber?
voor finss deh en DEWK-tee bahr-BEHR?

927. I want a haircut (shave).
Jeg skal klippes (barberes).
yay skahl KLIP-ess (bahr-BAY-ress).

928. Not too short.
Ikke for kort.
IK-eh fawr KAWRT.

929. Do not cut any off the top.
Ikke klipp av hårtoppene.
IK-eh KLIP ahv HAWR-tawp-eh-neh.

930. Do not put on oil.
Bruk ikke olje.
BREWK IK-eh AWL-yeh.

931. I part my hair on the (other) side.
Jeg har hårskillet på denne (andre) siden.
yay hahr HAWR-SHIL-eh paw DEN-eh (AHN-dreh) SEE-den.

932. The water is too hot (cold).
Vannet er for varmt (kaldt).
VAHN-eh är fawr VAHRMT (KAHLT).

933. I want my shoes shined.
Jeg vil ha pusset skoene mine.
yay vil hah PEWSS-et SKOO-eh-neh MEEN-eh.

934. Can I make an appointment for ——?
Kan jeg bestille time for ——?
kahn yay beh-STIL-eh TEEM-eh fawr ——?

935. I should like a new hair style.
Jeg vil gjerne ha ny hårfrisyre.
yay vil YÄR-neh hah NEW HAWR-free-SEW-reh.

936. I want to have my hair tinted (bleached).
Jeg vil ha håret lett farget (avfarget).
yay vil hah HAWR-eh let FAHR-get (ahv-FAHR-get).

937. May I see the color samples?
Må jeg se fargeprøvene, takk?
maw yay SEH FAHR-geh-PRER-veh-neh, tahk?

938. Beauty parlor. Frisørsalong, *m.*
free-SERR-sah-lawng.

939. Manicure. Håndpleie, *m.*
HAWN-play-eh.

940. A finger wave.   En ondulering.
en awn-dew-LEH-ring.

941. A shampoo.   En hårvask.
en HAWR-vahsk.

942. A permanent wave.   Permanentkrøller.
pehr-mah-NENT-KRERL-ehr.

943. A facial.   En ansiktsbehandling.
en AHN-sikts-beh-HAHN-ling.

944. A massage.   En massasje.
en mah-SAH-sheh.

945. Where can I find a chiropodist?
Hvor kan jeg finne en fotspesialist?
*voor kahn yay FIN-eh en FOOT-speh-see-ah-
LIST?*

**946. May I have an appointment for tomorrow
afternoon?**
Kan jeg bestille time for i morgen ettermid-
dag?
*kahn yay beh-STIL-eh TEEM-eh fawr ee-
MAWRN ET-ehr-mid-dah?*

PHOTOGRAPHY

FOTOGRAFI

947. I want a roll of (color) film.
Jeg vil ha en rull (farge) film.
yay vil hah en REWL (FAHR-geh) film.

948. For this camera.
For dette apparatet.
fawr DET-eh ah-pah-RAH-teh.

949. Movie film.   The size is ——.

Film.   Størrelsen er ——.

Film.   ST̄ER-rel-sen är ——.

950. What is the charge for developing a roll?

Hva koster det å framkalle en film?

vah KAWST-ehr deh aw FRAHM-kal-eh en FILM?

951. For one print of each.   Flashbulbs.

For hvert bilde.   Fotopære.

fawr VĀRT BEEL-deh.   FOO-TOO-pär-eh.

952. For an enlargement.

For en forstørrelse.

fawr en fawr-STĒR-rel-seh.

953. When will they be ready?

Når blir de ferdige?

nawr bleer de FĀR-ee-eh?

954. The camera is out of order.

Dette apparatet er i ustand.

DET-eh ah-pah-RAH-teh är ee EW-stahn.

955. Do you rent cameras?

Leier De ut fotografiapparater?

LAY-ehr dee EWT foo-too-GRAH-fee-ah-pah-RAH-tehr?

956. I should like one for today.

Jeg vil gjerne ha ett for i dag.

yay vil YĀR-neh hah et fawr ee-DAH.

957. Would you mind letting me take your picture?

Har De noe imot at jeg tar et fotografi av Dem?

hahr dee NOO-eh ee-MOOT aht yay TAHR et foo-too-GRAH-fee ahv dem?

LAUNDRY AND DRY CLEANING

VASKERI OG KJEMISK RENSING

958. Where is the nearest laundry (dry cleaner)?
Hvor er det nærmeste vaskeriet (renseriet)?
voor är deh NÅR-mest-eh vahsk-eh-REE-eh (ren-seh-REE-eh)?

959. I want this shirt to be washed (mended).
Jeg vil ha denne skjorten vasket (reparert).
yay vil hah DEN-eh SHOOR-ten VAHS-ket (reh-pah-REHRT).

960. Can you have this suit cleaned (pressed)?
Kan De rense (presse) denne dressen?
kahn dee REN-seh (PRESS-eh) DEN-eh DRESS-en?

961. Do not wash this in hot water.
Vask ikke denne her i varmt vann.
vahsk IK-eh DEN-eh här ee VAHRMT VAHN.

962. Use lukewarm water.
Bruk lunkent vann.
brewk LOONK-ent VAHN.

963. Be very careful.
Vær meget forsiktig.
vär MEH-get fawr-SHEEK-tee.

964. Remove this stain.
Ta bort denne flekken.
TAH boort DEN-eh FLEK-en.

965. Do not dry this in the sun.
Tørr ikke denne her i sola.
TERR IK-eh DEN-er här ee SOO-lah.

966. (Do not) starch the collars.
Stiv (ikke) snippene.
STEEV (IK-eh) SNIP-eh-neh.

967. When will it be ready?
Når blir det ferdig?
NAWR bleer deh FÄR-ee?

968. The belt is missing.
Beltet mangler.
BELT-eh MAHNG-lehr.

CLOTHING

KLÆR

969. An apron. Et forkle. *et FAWR-kleh.*

970. A bathing cap. En badehette.
en BAH-deh-HET-eh.

971. A bathing suit. En badedrakt.
en BAH-deh-DRAHKT.

972. Blouse. En bluse. *en BLEW-seh.*

973. Brassiere. En bysteholder.
en BEWST-eh-HAWL-ehr.

974. Coat (for men). En frakk.
en FRAHK.

975. Coat (for women). En kåpe.
en KAW-peh.

976. Collar. En snipp. *en SNIP.*

977. Collar pin. En snippnål. *en SNIP-nawl.*

978. Cuff links. Mansjettknapper.
mahn-CHET-knahp-ehr.

979. Diapers. Bleier. *BLAY-ehr*.

980. Dress. En kjole. *en CHOO-leh*.

981. Dressing gown. En slåbrok.
en SLAW-brawk.

982. Evening dress. Aftenkjole, *m.*
AHF-ten-CHOO-leh.

983. Garters. Sokkeholdere.
SAWK-keh-hawl-eh-reh.

984. Girdle. En hofteholder.
en HAWF-teh-hawl-er.

985. Gloves. Hansker. *HAHN-sker*.

986. Handkerchief. Et lommetørkle.
et LOOM-eh-TĒR-kleh.

987. Hat. En hatt. *en HAHT*.

988. Jacket. En jakke. *en YAHK-eh*.

989. Lapel. Oppslag, *n.* *AWP-shlahg*.

990. Necktie. Et slips. *et SHLEEPS*.

991. Nightgown. En nattkjole.
en NAHT-CHOO-leh.

992. Overcoat. En ytterfrakk.
en ĒWT-ehr-FRAHK.

993. Pajamas. Pyjamas, *c.* *pew-YAH-mahs*.

994. Panties. Underbenklær.
EWN-ehr-ben-KLÄR.

995. Petticoat. Underkjole, *c.*
EWN-ehr-CHOO-leh.

996. Raincoat (man's). Regnfrakk, *c.*
RAYN-FRAHK.

997. Raincoat (lady's). Regnkåpe, *c.*
RAYN-kaw-peh.

998. Robe. En badekåpe. *en BAH-deh-kaw-peh.*

999. Sandals (beach.) Sandaler (badesko).
sahn-DAH-lehr (BAH-deh-skoo).

1000. Scarf. Et skjerf. *et chärf.*

1001. Shirt. En skjorte. *en SHOORT-eh.*

1002. Shoes. Sko, *c. skoo.*

1003. Shorts. Shorts. *Shorts (as in English).*

1004. Skirt. Et skjørt. *et chērt.*

1005. Slacks. Slengbukser.
SLENG-BOOK-sehr.

1006. Slip. En underkjole.
en EWN-ehr-CHOO-leh.

1007. Slippers. Tøfler. *TĒRF-lehr.*

1008. Socks. Sokker. *SAWK-ehr.*

1009. Sport shirt. En sportsskjorte.
en SPOORTS-shoor-teh.

1010. Stockings (nylon). Strømper (nylon).
STRĒRM-pehr (NĒW-lawn).

1011. Suit. En dress. *en DRESS.*

1012. Suspenders. bukseseler.
BOOK-seh-sel-ehr.

1013. Sweater. En ullgenser.
en EWL-gen-sehr.

1014. Tiepin. Slipsnål, *m. SHLEEPS-nawl.*

1015. Trousers. Bukser. *BOOK-sehr.*

1016. Tuxedo. Smoking, *c.* *SMOO-king.*

1017. Undershirt. Underskjorte.
EWN-ehr-SHOOR-teh.

1018. Underwear. Undertøy. *EWN-ehr-TOY.*

1019. Vest. En vest. *en vest.*

HEALTH AND ACCIDENTS

HELSE OG ULYKKER

1020. What is the matter with you?
Hva feiler det Dem?
vah FAY-lehr deh dem?

1021. There has been an accident.
Det har hendt en ulykke.
deh hahr HENT en EW-LEW-keh.

1022. Get a doctor (nurse).
Hent en doktor (sykepleierske).
HENT en DAWK-toor (SEWK-eh-PLAY-ehr-skeh).

1023. Send for an ambulance.
Send bud etter en ambulanse.
SEN bew ET-ter en AHM-bew-LAHN-seh.

1024. Please bring blankets.
Bring ulltepper, takk.
bring EWL-tep-ehr, tahk.

1025. A stretcher.
En sykebåre.
en SEW-keh-BAW-reh.

1026. He is (seriously) injured.
Han er (alvorlig) skadet.
hahn är (ahl-VAWR-lee) SKAH-det.

1027. Help me carry him.
Hjelp meg bære ham.
YÄLP may BÄR-eh hahm.

1028. He was knocked down.
Han var blitt overkjørt.
hahn vahr blit AW-vehr-CHE̅RT.

1029. She fell (has fainted).
Hun falt (har besvimt).
he̅wn FAHLT (hahr beh-SVIMT).

1030. I feel weak. Wate..
Jeg føler meg dårlig. Vann, n.
yay FE̅R-lehr may DAW-lee. VAHN.

1031. He has a fracture (bruise, cut).
Han har et brudd (et skrapsår, et sår).
hahn hahr et BREWD (et SKRAHP-sawr, et SAWR).

1032. He has burned (cut) his hand.
Han har brent (skåret) seg i handa.
hahn hahr BRENT (SKAW-ret) say ee HAHN-ah.

1033. It is bleeding.
Det blør.
deh BLE̅RR.

1034. It is swollen.
Den er hovnet opp.
den är HAWV-net AWP.

1035. Can you dress this?
Kan De forbinde dette her?
kahn dee fawr-BIN-eh DET-eh här?

1036. Have you bandages or splints?
Har De bandasjer eller spjelk?
hahr dee bahn-DAH-shehr EL-lehr SPYELK?

1037. I need something for a tourniquet.
Har De noe for en turniket (OR: årepresse)?
*hahr dee NOO-eh fawr en tewr-nee-KEH OR:
AW-reh-press-eh)?*

1038. Are you all right?
Føler De Dem bra?
FĒR-lehr dee dem BRAH?

1039. It hurts here.
Det gjør vondt her.
deh YERR VOONT här.

1040. I want to sit down a moment.
Jeg vil sette meg ned et øyeblikk.
yay vil SET-eh may neh et OY-eh-BLIK.

1041. I cannot move my ——.
Jeg kan ikke røre —— min.
yay kahn IK-eh RĒR-reh —— meen.

1042. I have hurt my ——.
Jeg har skadet —— min.
yay hahr SKAH-det —— meen.

1043. Please notify my husband (wife, friend).
Vennligst underrett min mann (kone, venn).
*VEN-leegst EWN-ehr-et meen MAHN (KOO-
neh, VEN).*

1044. Here is my identification (my card).
Her er mitt kjennemerke (mitt visittkort).
här är mit CHEN-neh-MÄRK-eh (mit vee-SIT-koort).

1045. I have broken my glasses.
Brillene mine har gått i stykker.
BRIL-eh-neh MEEN-eh HAHR GAWT ee STEWK-ehr.

1046. I have lost my glasses.
Jeg har mistet brillene.
yay hahr MIST-et BRIL-eh-neh.

1047. Where can I find an optometrist?
Hvor kan jeg finne en øyenlege?
voor kan yay FIN-eh en OY-en-LEH-geh?

1048. Who can fix this hearing aid?
Hvem kan reparere dette høreapparatet?
VEM kahn reh-pah-RAY-reh DET-eh HER-reh-ah-pah-RAH-teh?

ILLNESS

SYKDOM

1049. I wish to see a doctor (specialist).
Jeg ønsker å se en doktor (spesialist).
yay ERN-skehr aw seh en DAWK-toor (SPEH-see-ah-LIST).

1050. An American doctor.
En amerikansk doktor.
en ah-meh-ree-KAHNSK DAWK-toor.

1051. I do not sleep well.
Jeg sover ikke bra.
yay SAW-vehr IK-eh BRAH.

1052. My foot hurts.
Det gjør vondt i foten min.
deh YERR VOONT ee FOO-ten meen.

1053. My head aches.
Jeg har hodepine.
yay hahr HOO-deh-pee-neh.

1054. I have a virus.
Jeg har virus.
yay hahr VEE-rewss.

1055. Can you give me something to relieve the pain?
Har De noe som kan lindre smertene?
hahr dee NOO-eh sawm kahn LIN-dreh SMÄRT-eh-neh?

1056. Appendicitis. Blindtarm, *c.*
BLIN-tahrm.

1057. Biliousness. Gallesyke, *c.*
GAHL-eh-SEW-keh.

1058. A bite. Et bitt. *et bit.*

1059. An insect bite. Et insektsbitt.
et IN-sekts-BIT.

1060. A blister. En blemme. *en BLEM-meh.*

1061. Blood pressure. Blodtrykk, *n.*
BLOO-trewk.

1062. A boil. En byll. *en bewl.*

1063. A burn. Et brannsår. *et BRAHN-sawr.*

1064. Chills. Frysninger. *FREWSS-ning-er.*

1065. A cold. En forkjølelse.
en fawr-CHERL-el-seh.

1066. Constipation. Forstoppelse, *m.*
fawr-SHTAWP-el-seh.

1067. A cough. En hoste. *en HOOSS-teh.*

1068. A cramp. En krampe. *en KRAHM-peh.*

1069. Diarrhœa. Diarré (OR: mavesyke), *c.*
dee-ah-RAY (OR: *MAH-veh-SEW-keh*).

1070. Dysentery. Dysenteri (OR: blodgang).
dew-sen-teh-REE (OR: *BLOO-gahng*).

1071. Earache. Øreverk, *n.*
ĒR-reh-VÄRK.

1072. A fever. En feber. *en FEH-behr.*

1073. Food poisoning. Matforgiftning, *c.*
MAHT-fawr-yift-ning.

1074. Hay fever. Høysnue, *c.* *HOY-snew-eh.*

1075. Hoarseness. Heshet, *c.* *HAYSS-het.*

1076. Indigestion. Dårlig fordøyelse, *c.*
DAW-lee fawr-DOY-el-seh.

1077. Nausea. Kvalme, *c.* *KVAHL-meh.*

1078. Pneumonia. Lungebetennelse, *c.*
LOON-geh-beh-TAYN-el-seh.

1079. A rash. Et utslett. *et EWT-shlet.*

1080. Sore throat. Vondt i halsen.
VOONT ee HAHL-sen.

1081. Chafed. Gnagsår (OR: hudirritasjon).
GNAHG-sawr (OR: *HEWD-ee-ree-tah-
SHOON*).

1082. Rheumatism. Gikt, *m.* *YEEKT.*

1083. Sprain. Forstuing, c. *fawr-STEW-ing.*

1084. Sunburned. Solbrent. *SOOL-brent.*

1085. Sunstroke. Solstikk, n. *SOOL-stik.*

1086. Typhoid fever. Tyfus. *TĒW-fewss.*

1087. An ulcer. Et magesår.
et MAH-geh-SAWR.

1088. To vomit. Å kaste opp. *aw KAHST-eh
awp.*

1089. What am I to do?
Hva skal jeg gjøre?
vah skahl yay YĒR-reh?

1090. Must I stay in bed?
Må jeg holde sengen?
MAW yay HAWL-eh SENG-en?

1091. Do I have to go to a hospital?
Må jeg på sjukhuset?
MAW yay paw SHEWK-hew-seh?

1092. May I get up?
Kan jeg stå opp?
kahn yay STAW AWP?

1093. I feel better.
Jeg føler meg bedre.
yay FĒR-lehr may BEH-dreh.

1094. When do you think I'll be better?
Når tror De jeg vil bli bedre?
nawr TROOR dee yay vil blee BEH-dreh?

1095. Can I travel on Monday?
Kan jeg reise mandag?
kahn yay RAY-seh MAHN-dah?

1096. When will you come again?
Når kommer De igjen?
nawr KAWM-ehr dee ee-YEN?

1097. Please send me a medical bill.
Vennligst send meg legeregningen.
VEN-leegst sen may LEH-geh-RAY-ning-en.

1098. Get well soon!
God bedring!
GOO BEH-dring.

1099. A drop. En dråpe. *en DRAW-peh.*

1100. A teaspoonful. En full teskje.
en FEWL teh-CHEH.

1101. Medicine. Medisin, *c. med-ee-SEEN:*

1102. Twice a day. To ganger daglig.
too GAHNG-ehr DAHG-lee.

1103. Hot water. Varmt vann.
VAHRMT vahn.

1104. Ice. Is. *eess.*

1105. A pill. En pille. *en PIL-leh.*

1106. A prescription. En resept.
en reh-SEPT.

1107. Every hour. Hver time. *vår TEE-meh.*

1108. Before (after) meals.
Før (etter) måltidet.
FERR (ET-tehr) MAWL-tee-eh.

1109. On going to bed. Før sengetid.
FERR SENG-eh-tee.

1110. On getting up. Når De står opp.
  nawr dee STAWR AWP.

1111. X-rays. Røntgen. *RĒRNT-gen.*

See also DRUGSTORE, page 104.

AT THE DENTIST'S

HOS TANNLEGEN

1112. I have a toothache.
  Jeg har tannpine.
  yay hahr TAHN-pee-neh.

1113. Do you know a good dentist?
  Vet De om en dyktig tannlege?
  VET dee awm en DĒWK-tee TAHN-leh-geh?

1114. This tooth hurts.
  Denne tanna gjør vondt.
  DEN-eh TAHN-eh YĒRR VOONT.

1115. Can you fix it temporarily?
  Kan De gi meg en foreløbig behandling?
  kahn dee yee may en FAW-reh-lēr-bee beh-HAHN-ling?

1116. I have lost a filling.
  Jeg har mistet en plombe.
  yay hahr MIST-et en PLAWM-beh.

1117. I have an abscess.
  Jeg har en byll.
  yay hahr en BĒWL.

1118. I have broken a tooth.
  Jeg har brukket en tann.
  yay hahr BREWK-et en TAHN.

1119. I (do not) want it extracted.
Jeg vil (ikke) ha den trukket ut.
yay vil (IK-eh) hah den TROOK-et EWT.

1120. Can you save it?
Kan De redde den?
kahn dee RED-eh den?

1121. You are hurting me.
Det gjør vondt.
deh YERR VOONT.

1122. Can you repair this denture?
Kan De reparere dette gebisset?
kahn dee reh-pah-RAY-reh DET-eh geh-BISS-eh?

1123. Local anesthesia.
Lokalbedøvelse.
loo-KAHL-beh-DERV-el-seh.

1124. Front tooth. Molar.
Fortann, *m.* Jeksel, *m.*
FAWR-tahn. YEK-sel.

1125. The gums. The nerve.
Gommene. Nerven.
GOOM-eh-neh. NÅR-ven.

DRUGSTORE

ET APOTEK

1126. Where is there a drugstore where they understand English?
Fins det et apotek hvor de forstår engelsk?
FINSS deh et ah-poo-TEK voor dee fawr-STAWR ENG-elsk?

1127. Can you fill this prescription?
Vil De ekspedere denne resepten?
*vil dee eks-peh-DEH-reh DEN-eh reh-SEP-
ten?*

1128. How long will it take?
Hvor lang tid vil det ta?
voor LAHNG tee vil deh tah?

1129. Can you deliver it to this address?
Kan De bringe den til denne adressen?
*kahn dee BRING-eh den til DEN-eh ah-DRESS-
en?*

1130. I want adhesive tape.
Jeg vil ha plaster.
yay vil hah PLAHSS-tehr.

1131. Alcohol. Alkohol. *ahl-koo-HOOL.*

1132. Antiseptic. Antiseptisk.
ahn-tee-SEP-tisk.

1133. Aspirin. Aspirin, *n.* *AHSS-pee-reen.*

1134. An analgesic. Et smertestillende middel.
et SMÄRT-eh-stil-en-neh MID-el.

1135. Bandages. Bandasjer. *bahn-DAH-sher.*

1136. Bicarbonate of soda. Bikarbonat, *n.*
BEE-kahr-boo-naht.

1137. Boric acid. Borsyre, *c.* *boor-SEW-reh.*

1138. A hair (tooth) brush.
En hår- (tann-) børste.
en HAWR- (TAHN-) BERSH-teh.

1139. Carbolic acid. Karbolsyre, *c.*
kahr-BOOL-sew-reh.

1140. Castor oil. Amerikansk olje, *c.*
ah-meh-ree-KAHNSK AWL-yeh.

1141. Cold cream. Koldkrem, *c.*
KAWL-krem.

1142. A comb. En kam. *en KAHM.*

1143. Corn pads. Liktornsplaster, *n.*
LEEK-toorns-plahss-tehr.

1144. Cotton. Bomull, *c.* *boom-EWL.*

1145. A depilatory. Hårfjerningsmiddel, *n.*
HAWR-fyär-ningss-MID-el.

1146. A deodorant. Et svettemiddel.
et SVET-eh-MID-el.

1147. Ear stoppers. Ørepropper.
ĒR-reh-PRAWP-ehr.

1148. Epsom salts. Epsomsalt.
EP-sawm-SAHLT.

1149. An eyecup. Et øyeglass.
et OY-eh-GLAHSS.

1150. Tissues. Papirtørklær.
pah-PEER-terr-KLÄR.

1151. A gargle. Et gurglevann.
et GEWR-gleh-VAHN.

1152. Gauze. Gasbind. *GAHSS-bin.*

1153. Hot water bottle. Varmtvannsflaske, *c.*
VAHRMT-vahnss-FLAHSK-eh.

1154. An icebag. En ispose. *en EESS-poo-seh.*

1155. Insect bite lotion OR: **Insect repellent.**
Myggolje, *c.* *MEWG-AWL-yeh.*

1156. Iodine. Jod, *c.* *YOOD.*

1157. A laxative (mild).
Et (mildt) avføringsmiddel.
et (milt) AHV-fer-ringss-MID-el.

1158. Lipstick. Lepestift, *c.* *LEP-eh-STIFT.*

1159. Medicine dropper. Medisindropper, *c.*
meh-dee-SEEN-drawp-er.

1160. Mouthwash. Munnvann, *n.*
MEWN-vahn.

1161. Nail file. Neglefil, *c.* *NAY-leh-feel.*

1162. Nail polish (remover).
Neglelakk (-fjerner), *m.*
NAY-leh-LAHK (-FYÄR-nehr).

1163. Peroxide. Peroksyd, *c.* *peh-rawk-SEWD.*

1164. Powder. Pudder, *n.* *PEW-dehr.*

1165. Poison. Gift, *c.* *yift.*

1166. Quinine. Kinin, *c.* *kee-NEEN.*

1167. A razor. En barberhøvel.
en bahr-BEHR-her-vel.

1168. Razor blades. Barberblar.
bahr-BEHR-blahr.

1169. Rouge. Rouge (OR: Rød sminke).
rewsh (OR: rer SMEENK-eh).

1170. Sanitary napkins. Damebind, *n.*
DAHM-eh-bin.

1171. A sedative. Et beroligende middel.
et beh-ROOH-lee-en-eh MID-el.

1172. Shampoo (liquid, cream).
Hårvask (veske, krem), *c.*
HAWR-vahsk (VESK-eh, krem).

1173. Shaving lotion. Barbervann, *n.*
bahr-BEHR-vahn.

1174. Shaving cream (brushless).
Barberkrem, *c.* (Skumfri).
bahr-BEHR-krem (SKEWM-free).

1175. A bar of soap. Et såpestykke.
et SAW-peh-STEWK-eh.

1176. Soap flakes. Såpespon, *n.*
SAW-peh-spoon.

1177. Sunburn ointment.
Salve mot solbrenthet.
SAHL-veh moot SOOL-brent-het.

1178. Smelling salts. Luktesalt, *n.*
LOOK-teh-sahlt.

1179. Suntan oil. Solbadolje, *c.*
SOOL-bahd-AWL-yeh.

1180. A thermometer. Et termometer.
et tär-moo-MEH-tehr.

1181. Toilet tissue. Toalettpapir, *n.*
too-ah-LET-pah-PEER.

1182. Toothpaste. Tannpasta, *c.*
TAHN-PAHSS-tah.

1183. Toothpowder. Tannpulver, *n.*
TAHN-pewl-vehr.

COMMUNICATIONS: TELEPHONE

SAMBAND: TELEFON

1184. A telephone directory.
En telefonkatalog.
en teh-leh-FOON-kah-tah-LAWG.

1185. Where can I telephone?
Hvor kan jeg telefonere?
voor kahn yay teh-leh-foo-NEH-reh?

1186. Will you telephone for me?
Vil De telefonere for meg?
vil dee teh-leh-foo-NEH-reh fawr may?

1187. I want to make a local call, number ——.
Jeg vil ha en lokalsamtale, nummer ——.
yay vil hah en loo-KAHL sahm-tah-leh,
NOOM-ehr ——.

1188. Give me the long distance operator.
La meg få rikstelefonen, frøken.
lah may faw RIKS-teh-leh-FOON-en, FRÖR-ken.

1189. The operator will call you.
Telefondamen vil ringe Dem.
teh-leh-FOON-dahm-en vil RING-eh dem.

1190. I want number ——.
Jeg vil ha nummer ——.
yay vil hah NOOM-ehr ——.

1191. They do not answer.
De svarer ikke.
dee SVAHR-ehr IK-eh.

1192. The line is busy.
Linjen er opptatt.
LEEN-yen är AWP-taht.

1193. Hold the line, please.
Ikke bryt forbindelsen.
IK-eh BREWT fawr-BIN-el-sen.

1194. May I speak to ——?
Får jeg snakke med ——?
fawr yay SNUK-eh meh ——?

1195. He is not present.
Han er ikke til stede.
hahn är IK-eh til-STEH-deh.

1196. This is —— speaking.
Dette er ——.
DET-eh är——.

1197. Please take a message for ——.
Vær så snill å ta en beskjed for ——.
vär saw snil aw tah en beh-SHEH fawr ——.

1198. My number is ——.
Mitt nummer er ——.
mit NOOM-er är ——.

1199. How much is a call to ——?
Hva koster en samtale til ——?
vah KAWST-ehr en SAHM-tah-leh til ——?

1200. There is a telephone call for you.
Det er telefon til Dem.
deh är teh-leh-FOON til dem.

USEFUL INFORMATION: DAYS OF THE WEEK

NYTTIGE OPPLYSNINGER: UKEDAGER

1201. Sunday. Søndag. *SERN-dah.*

1202. Monday. Mandag. *MAHN-dah.*

1203. Tuesday. Tirsdag. *TEESH-dah.*

1204. Wednesday. Onsdag. *OONSS-dah.*

1205. Thursday. Torsdag. *TAWSH-dah.*

1206. Friday. Fredag. *FREH-dah.*

1207. Saturday. Lørdag. *LERR-dah.*

MONTHS, SEASONS AND WEATHER
MÅNEDER, ÅRSTIDER OG VÆR

1208. January. Januar. *yah-new-AHR.*

1209. February. Februar. *feh-brew-AHR.*

1210. March. Mars. *mahsh.*

1211. April. April. *ah-PREEL.*

1212. May. Mai. *MAH-ee.*

1213. June. Juni. *YEW-nee.*

1214. July. Juli. *YEW-lee.*

1215. August. August. *erv-GEWST.*

1216. September. September. *sep-TEM-behr.*

1217. October. Oktober. *ook-TOO-behr.*

1218. November. November. *noo-VEM-behr.*

1219. December. Desember. *deh-SEM-behr.*

1220. Fall. Høst, *c.* *hersht.*

1221. Winter. Vinter, *c.* *VIN-tehr.*

1222. Spring. Vår, *c.* *vawr.*

1223. Summer. Sommer, *c.* *SAWM-ehr.*

HOLIDAYS

HELLIGDAGER

1224. Christmas. Jul, c. *yewl.*

1225. Whitsun. Pinse, c. *PIN-seh.*

1226. Easter. Påske, c. *PAW-skeh.*

1227. Good Friday. Langfredag, c. *LAHNG-freh-dah.*

1228. Lent. Faste, c. *FAHSS-teh.*

1229. New Year's Day. Nyttårsdag, c. *NEWT-aws-dah.*

1230. Legal Holiday. Lovfestete helligdager. *LAWV-FEST-eh-teh HEL-ee-dah-ehr.*

TIME AND TIME EXPRESSIONS

TID OG TIDSUTTRYKK

Note.—In Norway the clock runs from 1 to 24 (EXAMPLE: 1 P.M. is 13; 12 midnight is 24).

1231. What time is it?
Hva er klokka?
vah ǎr KLUK-ah?

1232. It is two o'clock A.M. (P.M.).
Klokka er to (fjorten).
KLUK-ah ǎr TOO (FYOOR-ten).

1233. It is half-past four.
Den er halv fem (half hours are counted before the hour).
den ǎr hahl fem.

1234. It is a quarter past ——.
Den er kvart over ——.
den är kvahrt AW-vehr ——.

1235. It is a quarter to ——.
Den er kvart på ——.
den är kvahrt paw ——.

1236. At ten minutes to ——.
Ti minutter på ——.
tee min-EWT-ehr paw ——.

1237. At ten minutes past ——.
Ti minutter over ——.
tee min-EWT-ehr AW-vehr ——.

1238. In the morning.
Om morgenen.
awm MAWR-eh-nen.

1239. In the evening.
Om aftenen (OR: kvelden).
awm AHF-teh-nen (OR: KVEL-en).

1240. In the afternoon.
Om ettermiddagen.
awm ET-tehr-MEE-dah-en.

1241. At noon. Klokka tolv.
KLUK-ah TAWL.

1242. Day. Dag, *c. dah.*

1243. Night. Natt, *c. naht.*

1244. Midnight. Midnatt, *c. MEED-naht.*

1245. The midnight sun. Midnattsolen.
MEED-naht-SOOL-en.

1246. Yesterday. I går. *ee-GAWR.*

1247. Last night. I går kveld.
ee-GAWR kvel.

1248. Today. I dag. *ee-DAH.*

1249. Tonight. I natt. *ee-NAHT.*

1250. Tomorrow. I morgen. *ee-MAWRN.*

1251. Last year. I fjor. *ee-FYOOR.*

1252. Last month. Forrige måned.
FAWR-ree-eh MAW-neh.

1253. Next Monday. Neste mandag.
NEST-eh MAHN-dah.

1254. Next week. Neste uke.
NEST-eh-EWK-eh.

1255. The day before yesterday. I forgårs.
ee FAWR-GAWSH.

1256. The day after tomorrow.
I overmorgen. *ee AW-vehr-MAWRN.*

1257. Two weeks ago. For to uker siden.
fawr TOO EWK-ehr SEE-den.

1258. One week ago. For en uke siden.
fawr en EWK-eh SEE-den.

NUMBERS: CARDINALS

GRUNNTALL

1259. 0. **Zero.** Null. *newl.*

1. **One.** En (OR: ett). *en* (OR: *et*).

2. **Two.** To. *too.*

3. **Three.** Tre. *treh.*

4. **Four.** Fire. *FEE-reh.*

5. **Five.** Fem. *fem.*
6. **Six.** Seks. *seks.*
7. **Seven.** Sju (OR: syv).
   shew (OR: *sewv*).
8. **Eight.** Åtte. *AWT-teh.*
9. **Nine.** Ni. *nee.*
10. **Ten.** Ti. *tee.*
11. **Eleven.** Elleve. *EL-eh-veh.*
12. **Twelve.** Tolv. *tawl.*
13. **Thirteen.** Tretten. *TRET-ten.*
14. **Fourteen.** Fjorten. *FYOOR-ten.*
15. **Fifteen.** Femten. *FEM-ten.*
16. **Sixteen.** Seksten. *SAY-sen.*
17. **Seventeen.** Sytten. *SĒRT-ten.*
18. **Eighteen.** Atten. *AHT-ten.*
19. **Nineteen.** Nitten. *NEET-ten.*
20. **Twenty.** Tjue (OR: tyve).
    CHEW-eh (OR: *TĒW-veh*).
21. **Twenty-one.** Tjue en.
    CHEW-eh-en.
22. **Twenty-two.** Tjue to.
    CHEW-eh-too.
30. **Thirty.** Tretti. *TRĒT-tee.*
40. **Forty.** Førti. *FĒRR-tee.*
50. **Fifty.** Femti. *FEM-tee.*
60. **Sixty.** Seksti. *SEKS-tee.*
70. **Seventy.** Sytti. *SĒRT-tee.*
80. **Eighty.** Åtti. *AWT-tee.*
90. **Ninety.** Nitti. *NIT-tee.*
100. **One hundred.** Et hundre.
     et HEWN-dreh.

101. **One hundred and one.**
Et hundre og en. *et HEWN-dreh aw en.*

200. **Two hundred.** To hundre.
too HEWN-dreh.

1000. **One thousand.** Et tusen.
et TEWSS-en.

2000. **Two thousand.** To tusen.
too TEWSS-en.

NUMBERS: ORDINALS

ORDENSTALL

First. Først. *Fērst.*

Second. Annen (annet, andre).
AH-nen (AH-net; AHN-dreh).

Third. Tredje. *TREH-dyeh.*

Fourth. Fjerde. *FYÄR-eh.*

Fifth. Femte. *FEM-teh.*

Sixth. Sjette. *SHET̄-eh.*

Seventh. Sjuende. *SHEW-eh-neh.*

Eighth. Åttende. *AWT-eh-neh.*

Ninth. Niende. *NEE-eh-neh.*

Tenth. Tiende. *TEE-eh-neh.*

Eleventh. Ellevte. *EL-ef-teh.*

Twelfth. Tolvte. *TAWL-teh.*

Thirteenth. Trettende. *TRET-eh-neh.*

Fourteenth. Fjortende. *FYOOR-teh-neh.*

Fifteenth. Femtende. *FEM-teh-neh.*

Sixteenth. Sekstende. *SAYSS-eh-neh.*

Seventeenth. Syttende. *SĒRT-eh-neh.*

Eighteenth. Attende. *AHT-eh-neh.*

Nineteenth. Nittende. *NIT-eh-neh.*

Twentieth. Tjuende. *CHEW-eh-neh.*

Twenty-first. Tjueførste.
CHEW-eh-FERSS-teh.

Twenty-second. Tjueandre.
CHEW-eh-AHN-dreh.

Thirtieth. Trettiende.
TRAYT-ee-eh-neh.

MEASUREMENTS

MÅL

1260. What is the length (width)?
Hva er lengden (bredden)?
vah är LENG-den (BREH-den)?

1261. How much is it per meter?
Hva koster det per meter?
vah KAWST-eh deh pär MEH-tehr?

1262. Degree of latitude. Degree of longitude.
Breddegrad. Lengdegrad.
BREH-deh-grahd. LENG-deh-grahd.

1263. What is the size?
Hvilken størrelse er det?
VEEL-ken STERR-el-seh är deh?

1264. It is ten meters long by four meters wide.
Den er ti meter lang og fire meter bred.
den är TEE MEH-tehr LAHNG, aw FEE-reh MEH-tehr BREH.

1265. High. Høy. *hoy.*

1266. Low. Lav. *lahv.*

1267. Large. Stor. *stoor.*

1268. Medium. Mellomstor. *MEL-awm-STOOR.*

1269. Small. Liten. *LEE-ten.*

1270. Alike. lik. *leek.*

1271. Different. Ulik. *EW-leek.*

1272. A pair. Et par. *et pahr.*

1273. A dozen. Et dusin. *et dew-SEEN.*

1274. Half a dozen. Et halvt dusin. *et HAHLT dew-SEEN.*

1275. Half a meter. En halv meter. *en HAHL MEH-tehr.*

1276. Fractions. Brøker. *BRĒR-kehr.*

1277. One-half. En halvdel. *en HAHL-del.*

1278. One-third. En tredel. *en TREH-del.*

1279. One-fourth. En firedel. *en FEE-reh-del.*

1280. Three-fourths. Tre firedeler. *treh FEE-reh-del-ehr.*

COLORS

FARGER

1281. Light. Lys. *lēwss.*

1282. Dark. Mørk. *mērk.*

1283. Black. Sort. *soort.*

1284. Blue. Blå. *blaw.*

1285. Brown. Brun. *brewn.*

1286. Cream. Krem. *krem.*

1287. Green. Grønn. *grẽrn.*

1288. Orange. Oransje. *oh-RAHN-sheh.*

1289. Pink. Lyserød. *LEW̃-seh-rẽr.*

1290. Purple. Purpur. *PEWR-pewr.*

1291. Red. Rød. *rẽr.*

1292. White. Hvit. *veet.*

1293. Yellow. Gul. *gewl.*

1294. I want a lighter (darker) shade.
Jeg vil ha en lysere (mørkere) farge.
*yay vil hah en LEW̃-seh-reh (MẼRR-keh-reh)
FAHR-geh.*

COMMON OBJECTS

ALMINNELIGE GJENSTANDER

1295. Ashtray. Et askebeger.
et AHSK-eh-beg-ehr.

1296. Bobby pins. Hårnåler.
HAWR-nawl-ehr.

1297. Book shelf. En bokhylle.
en BOOK-hewl-eh.

1298. Bottle opener. En flaskeåpner.
en FLAHSK-eh-AWP-nehr.

1299. Box. En eske. *en ESS-keh.*

1300. Bulb (light). En lyspære
en LEW̃SS-pär-eh.

1301. Candy. Konfekt. *kawn-FEKT.*

1302. Can opener. En bokseåpner.
en BAWK-seh-AWP-nehr.

1303. Cleaning fluid. Et rensemiddel.
et REN-seh-MID-el.

1304. Cloth. Klær. *klär.*

1305. Clock. Ei klokke. *ay KLUK-eh.*

1306. Cork. En kork. *en kawrk.*

1307. Corkscrew. En korketrekker.
en KAWRK-eh-TREK-ehr.

1308. Curtains. Gardiner. *gahr-DEEN-ehr.*

1309. Cushion. En (sofa-) pute.
en (SOO-fah-) PEW-teh.

1310. Doll. Ei dukke. *ay DEWK-eh.*

1311. Earrings. Øreringer. *ĒR-reh-RING-er.*

1312. Flashlight. En lommelykt.
en LOOM-eh-LĒWKT.

1313. Glasses. Briller. *BRIL-ehr.*

1314. Sunglasses. Solbriller.
SOOL-bril-ehr.

1315. Gold. Gull, *n.* *gewl.*

1316. Chewing gum. Tyggegummi, *n.*
TEWG-eh-GEWM-ee.

1317. Hairnet. Hårnett, *n.* *HAWR-net.*

1318. Hook. En krok. *en krook.*

1319. Iron (flat). Et strykejern.
et STREWK-eh-yărn.

1320. Jewelry. Juveler. *yuh-VEL-ehr.*

1321. Leather. Et lær. *et lăr.*

1322. Linen. Et lintøy. *et LEEN-toy.*

1323. Lock. En lås. *en lawss.*

1324. Mirror. Et speil. *et spayl.*

1325. Mosquito net. Et moskitonett.
et moo-SKIH-too-net.

1326. Necklace. Et halsband.
et HAHLSS-bahn.

1327. Needle. En nål. *en nawl.*

1328. Notebook. En notisbok.
en noo-TEESS-book.

1329. Pail. Ei bøtte. *ay BER-teh.*

1330. Penknife. En lommekniv.
en LOOM-eh-KNEEV.

1331. Perfume. Parfyme, *c. pahr-FEW-meh.*

1332. Pillow. En pute. *en PEW-teh.*

1333. Pin (ornamental). En brosje.
en BRAW-sheh.

1334. Pin (safety). En sikkerhetsnål.
en SIK-kehr-hets-NAWL.

1335. Pin (straight). En knappnål.
en KNAHP-nawl.

1336. Pocketbook. En lommebok.
en LOOM-eh-BOOK.

1337. Purse. En pung. *en poong.*

1338. Radio. En radio. *en RAH-dee-oo.*

1339. Ring. En ring. *en ring.*

1340. Rubbers. Kalosjer. *kah-LAWSH-ehr.*

1341. Scissors. En saks. *en sahks.*

1342. Screw. En skru. *en skrew.*

1343. Shade. En rullegardin.
en REWL-leh-gahr-deen.

1344. Shoe polish. En skosverte.
en SKOO-svär-teh.

1345. Shoelace. En skolisse. *en SKOO-liss-eh.*

1346. Silk. Silke, *c. SEEL-keh.*

1347. Silver. Sølv, *n. se̅rl.*

1348. Sponge. En svamp. *en svahmp.*

1349. Stone (precious). En edelsten.
en EH-del-STEN.

1350. Stopper. En propp. *en prawp.*

1351. Strap. En rem. *en rem.*

1352. Straw. Et strå. *et straw.*

1353. Suitcase. En koffert. *en KOOF-ehrt.*

1354. Sweets. Et sukkertøy. *et SOOK-ehr-toy.*

1355. Thimble. Et fingerbøl. *et FING-ehr-BE̅RL.*

1356. Thread. En tråd. *en traw.*

1357. Toy. Et leketøy.
et LEH-keh-toy.

1358. Typewriter.   En skrivemaskin.
en SKREE-veh-MAH-sheen.

1359. Umbrella.   En paraply.   *en pah-rah-PLEW.*

1360. Vase.   En vase.   *en VAH-seh.*

1361. Watch.   Et armbåndsur.
et AHRM-bawnss-ewr.

1362. Whiskbroom.   En feiekost.
en FAY-eh-koost.

1363. Wire.   En ledning.   *en LED-ning.*

1364. Wood.   Tre, *n.   treh.*

1365. Wool.   Ull, *c.   ewl.*

1366. Zipper.   En glidelås.
en GLEE-deh-lawss.

INDEX

INDEX

The words in CAPITALS refer to sections, and the first number that follows (example: p. 81) refers to the page. Otherwise, ALL ENTRIES ARE INDEXED BY ITEM NUMBER.

127